DEAD MAN BREATHING

Without the dedication and bravery of five men, our story would have a much different ending. This book is dedicated to those men who lovingly risked their own lives to save mine the night of March 3, 2006. Because of that we are much appreciative and love each one of you. Thank you, my brothers of H&P 226: Adron "Bulldog" Brown, Billy Humble, Stephen "Shakey" Higgins, Michael "Tad" Gary, and Richard Horn.

BILLY JACK &
A'LETA MCDANIEL
WITH CAROLYN STANFORD GOSS AND LEONARD G. GOSS

DEAD MAN BREATHING

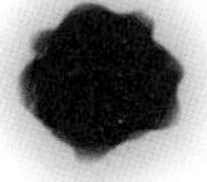

THE INCREDIBLE TRUE STORY OF
ONE MAN'S RISE FROM THE FLAMES

WinePressPublishing
Great Books, Defined.

2nd printing in 2013.

WinePress Publishing (PO Box 428, Enumclaw, WA 98022) functions only as book publisher. As such, the ultimate design, content, editorial accuracy, and views expressed or implied in this work are those of the author.

ISBN 13: 978-1-60615-217-1
ISBN 10: 1-60615-217-3
Library of Congress Catalog Card Number: 2011962732

Printed in China.

"Come a Little Closer"

(Used by Permission)

Lyrics and Music by Dierks Bentley*
(2005)

Come a little closer baby
I feel like layin' you down
On a bed of sweet surrender
Where we can work it all out.
There ain't nothin' that love can't fix,
Girl, it's right here at our finger tips;
So come a little closer baby
I feel like layin' you down.

Come a little closer baby
I feel like lettin' go
Of everything that stands between us
And the love we used to know.
I wanna touch you like a cleansing rain
And let it wash all the hurt away;
So come a little closer baby
I feel like lettin' go.

If there's still a chance,
Then take my hand
And we'll steal away,
Off into the night
Until we make things right.
The sun's gonna rise on a better day.

Come a little closer baby
I feel like strippin' it down,
Back to the basics of you and me
And what makes the world go round,
Every inch of you against my skin,
I wanna be stronger than we've ever been;
So come a little closer baby
I feel like strippin' it down.

Come a little closer baby
Just a little bit closer baby
Come a little closer baby
I feel like layin' you down.

CONTENT

FOREWORD

by Chris McDaniel,
Mississippi state senator (first cousin to Billy Jack)

Even now, years later, it's difficult to recall without sadness.

After Jack's wife, A'Leta, shared the tragic news that he had been injured during an explosion on a drilling rig in Texas, I knew I had to prepare myself for a difficult reality. But I had little idea of how harrowing the struggle would be, particularly for Jack, A'Leta, and their daughter, Carney.

I arrived at the burn center in Shreveport for the first time and was met by anxious family and friends while I was quickly prepared for my initial visit with him.

The pain caused as the result of a burn injury is well-known to most, as minor burns are a part of the human experience. But witnessing the unimaginable devastation caused to Jack's body—which had been burned on more than ninety-five percent of its surface area—was something I had never experienced.

Shrouded within darkness and alone in a small hospital room filled with a labyrinth of tubes, bandages, and machines, lay my first cousin. It was tough to see him, much less recognize him. It was even more difficult to understand how surviving such tragedy would even be possible. Bodily fluids leaked onto his linens, while the smell of death permeated his room. Suffering and hopelessness appeared to be his constant, unwelcome companions.

I had so many questions for him and far too much responsibility for the moment; my heart raced with anguish.

Though I attempted to initiate a conversation, Jack was not responsive. I told him not to worry, that I would take care of his family, but I was met with silence and despair. The machines around him continued to buzz and beep.

Leaving his room, stepping back into the light, I honestly did not expect Jack to live. I was certain I would not see him again, even though his wife kept reminding me—in an almost supernatural fashion—that he would survive his injuries. I prayed that God would bring peace and mercy to his suffering. I asked that he also spare his life, but I was preparing myself for his passing.

And yet, as days turned into weeks, Jack displayed the heart of a lion. His will to live was incredible as he was supported by a dedicated wife, beautiful daughter, and unyielding faith.

Jack had no intention of giving up and no expectation of dying.

It soon became apparent to everyone, including the doctors and nurses, that he was a living miracle. There was no plausible medical explanation as to how his survival was even possible, but those who knew the faith upon which he relied understood that God had a plan for him.

An immeasurable wealth of character was born and accumulated amid the fire of faith, love, honor, and courage.

For months, the state of Mississippi—friends and strangers alike—reached out to comfort the McDaniel family. In turn, Jack, A'Leta, and Carney used that support and their pain as the motivation to turn tragedy into triumph, glorifying their Savior instead of blaming Him for difficult conditions.

In watching their struggles, we have all been reminded that when we face the suffering of a loved one and impossible odds, we come face-to-face with the power of God.

There is no question in my mind that I witnessed a miracle.

This book tells their story.

—Chris McDaniel
Jackson, Mississippi
July 24, 2011

"FIRE ON THE RIG!"

Billy Jack McDaniel

"Explosion on the rig! Fire on the rig! I'm on fire!" My yells turned to screams that were instantly absorbed in the *whoosh* of flames engulfing my body.

I was harnessed up on a seventeen-foot-long platform about ninety feet above ground. When I saw the fire racing up toward me, I knew there was nothing I could do. I was in the fire's path, and I was going to be lit up like a torch. I had nowhere to go.

The flames burst up about 350 feet into the air. I was completely engulfed. Fighting the flames with my hands, I ran to the far-right corner of the platform. There were a couple of rows of pipe standing in the derrick. I tried to crawl behind the standing pipe to stop that fire from burning up the rest of me, but there was no place to hide and no time to plan.

The fire! Dear God, the fire! It was gorgeous—teal blues, glittering yellows, fluorescent oranges, ambers, reds. The flames lit up the black March sky like a roasting fire for a giant's kill. It swallowed me up in seconds, and I was the one roasting, my body cooking fast. It's amazing how something so beautiful can be so devastating.

"Shut it in, shut it in!" I screamed. From the corner I continued to slap myself, trying to get that fire off. I ran to the Geronimo line, which is an escape cable that runs from the derrick board down to the ground. It has a small T-bar on it that runs on pulleys, and a brass plate attached to the lever. You pull down, and it slows you down. It was tied to the derrick board. Everybody thought it was a great design—no problems—until you need to get away fast.

I was in such searing pain I couldn't get my fingers—raw and dripping flesh and fluids—to untie the T-bar. All I had to do was pull one rope, but it was like trying to thread a needle in the middle of a hornet's nest. I couldn't do it. Even if I had been able to untie it, I still had to crawl through the hand rails to get on it. There was no way I could do that.

I gave up in a few seconds and ran to the end of the board. I knew I was a dead man. I had to put myself out of this horrific pain and die quickly. The fire's long, red-and-orange plumes were still reaching upwards. I jumped and landed on my back on the platform.

The harness I was wearing went over my shoulders, across my back, and between my legs. I also wore a belly rope, about eight inches wide and two inches thick, that goes from hip to hip. You put it on, and that's your lever. As you pull the pipes, you have something to pull against. We were supposed to use something called a *lanyard*. It's nylon and has a spring-like feel that slows you down as it comes out. Our deck hands used a braided cable made out of eighth-inch steel. It was attached to the back hand rail where the lanyards were tied. We used that, and it was going to hurt when it stopped you, but you would stop. Great plan—except when it won't allow you to get away.

That's what snatched me back to the board the first time. I struggled to get up, and my left leg fell through the alleyway, between the board and the fingers. I put my right hand down to push myself up, and the palm of my hand was burned on contact. I got up, ran, and jumped again. I don't know how it happened, but I landed on my back again.

"God!" I yelled. "What's the deal?" There was no escape!

At this point, only seconds had passed. I was still beating myself, trying to get the fire off. Muscle and skin were flying in chunks and flakes. Then my hard hat began to melt. It dripped down my face, and fire fell from my head. I threw the hat away from my head, and it fell into the fire. It looked like when you throw a paper plate in a fireplace—it just went *shooop*. Later, they found the hat about 150 yards away from the rig, flattened and about as big as a saucer.

I don't know how I managed it, but I got up again. Amazingly, I could still walk, and what was left of Billy Jack McDaniel somehow made it to the ladder. I was going to jump. Falling to my death was better than living. That's how real it was.

Then the fire began to go out.

"WE DON'T KNOW HOW BAD HE IS BURNED"

A'Leta

"A'Leta, can you please open the door? Please! I'm in your driveway! I need to talk to you—now!"

It was exactly 12:03 a.m. on March 4, 2006, when Jack's district rig supervisor, Bob, called me on his cell from his truck. I had just gone to bed, and I thought Jack was calling. He'd called and spoken to Carney and me several times that day, more than usual. I wondered if something was wrong on the rig.

As soon as I realized Bob was calling me from the driveway, I knew something was very wrong. I hung up the phone and called my dad. "You've got to come to my house right now. I've got a problem." I hung up the phone and started crying a little. I picked out my clothes and put them on, but I didn't hurry—I was moving in a thick fog of shock and disbelief.

The phone rang again. "A'Leta, I'm at the door. Open up." When I opened the door, Bob and his wife, Mrs. Peggy, were standing there. I knew it wasn't good.

"Let's sit down and talk about this," Bob said.

They sat me down. "Just give me the facts," I told him.

"There was an explosion on the rig, and Jack was burned. We don't know yet how badly he was burned. We don't know anything except that he was burned. I don't know where he is or where they're taking him. Just go get some clothes and things, and we'll get in the truck and head west."

I got up off the couch, and that's when my daddy walked through the door. The look on his face was horrible. He was alone. His face was white. He said, "What happened?"

Bob answered, "Jack was burned, Lemuel."

"No!"

"Yeah," Bob said.

"How bad?" my daddy asked.

"I don't know. I just had a call that he was burned."

"No, no!" Daddy said. "He can't go through that!"

My daddy knew what it was like to be burned badly. He had been burned from the waist up more than thirty years ago. I could tell his memory of how bad it was came flooding back. He was immediately taken back to the horrific day at work that had changed his life forever.

Bob shook his head. "Yeah, I know."

Oddly enough, my first reaction to all of this was to feel bad for my daddy. I saw the emotion in his face. He was hurting for Jack as only one who has felt the same kind of pain can. I had never seen my daddy look like that, and it upset me.

I realized that Daddy knew more than he was saying. You know how daddies just know things sometimes? He must have known things were really bad because Bob was there. If it had been just a minor burn, they probably wouldn't have contacted me. For Mr. Bob to show up at this time of night, he knew. And my mama knew it was bad when he called her.

Daddy went to our bedroom, where Carney was sleeping (she always slept with us), and carried her out to his car. Bob and I got into the truck and left. A nurse called my cell as we were driving across I-20. "I'm the nurse from Nacogdoches Medical Center, Mrs. McDaniel. I have your husband here. He's been burned, and he said to tell you he loves you."

"How bad?"

"Really bad, ma'am. He's burned all over. He was brought into the emergency room screaming."

It may seem strange, but her call relieved me a little. I knew that if Jack was screaming, his lungs were working.

"I gave him a lot of medicine, and he's gonna be out pretty quick," the nurse told me.

"Will you tell him I love him?" I could hardly get the words out, but she said she would.

"Now, ma'am," she finished, "we're going to med flight him over to LSU in Shreveport. We'll probably be there in a couple of hours." She gave us the address, and that's where we went.

I had to make some calls while we were in the truck. Daddy had taken Carney to his and Mama's house, and I needed to tell them what I knew. I called our best friends, Shelly and Stephen Harrison.

When we arrived at the hospital, Mr. Bob dropped Mrs. Peggy and me off at the front door and I went in. What happened from this point on is sketchy in my memory. They told us to go to a room next to the ER, where I gave the sweet, southern lady in admissions Jack's personal information.

Meanwhile, Bob had parked the truck. He must have talked to the doctor on call while I was in the admissions office, which wasn't long at all. As soon as I walked out, Bob and a doctor came up to me. They were walking fast.

"I'm Dr. Sittig." He held out his hand. "I'm a burn specialist. Your husband's here. If you'll walk with me to the waiting room, I'll sit down with you and talk about it."

By now, I was just going through the motions. I remember him talking to me as we were walking down the hall, but I don't remember what he said.

Since Bob had already talked with Dr. Sittig, he knew more than I did about what was going on. He knew that it was bad. Dr. Sittig had told him that Billy Jack was pretty much dead, that there was nothing more they could do at this time.

"Mrs. McDaniel, please sit down," Dr. Sittig said. "Your husband has been burned over ninety-five percent of his body. I can't give you a lot of details yet. I've examined him, and they're bandaging him up. He is probably not going to live even twenty-four hours."

I stood up. "I've gotta see him!"

"When the nurses are finished, you can go back there and see him."

"Can you tell me anything about how he's doing?" I asked.

"He has three things going for him. He's young, and he's in good physical shape. And there's one more thing: God. Outside of that, there's nothing I can do. I've done what I can. If he survives seventy-two hours, I can start to work on him. But right now it's just wait and see."

"Do you believe in God?" I asked him.

"Yes, ma'am, I do."

"Do you believe he works miracles?"

"Yes."

"Well, Jack's not going to die. He's just not."

What Dr. Sittig said surprises me now when I think of it. He said, "I'm praying right along with you. You get everybody praying for him, and if God wants him to live, he'll live. If he doesn't, he's not gonna live. It's out of my control."

I wasn't upset. I never really got upset that much while I was at the hospital. Except for the first time I saw Jack, I did most of my crying when nobody was around—when I was by myself at the hotel. Even from the beginning I knew that if I did start to cry, it would not go away quickly. It would be an ongoing, long-term thing, and I did not want to be in that situation. I had to be on top of my game for Jack.

Jack was my "Baby," as I called him, but a *baby* he was not. Tough-skinned as a Mississippi armadillo, Jack seemed rough on the outside, but his love for me and our daughter, Carney, went way back, to when we were just teenagers. Here's his story, much of it in his own words—with mine thrown in from time to time.

FROM LONELY CHILD TO GOD'S CHILD

Billy Jack McDaniel

I was born in Laurel, Mississippi, to Jacky McDaniel and Hope Mercer McDaniel. I had a good early childhood up to about six years old. Then out of the blue one day, my mama decided to leave. I didn't understand why. I just knew she was gone.

My mom and dad had never argued. They never had a foul word with one another—so why she left was a mystery to me. Up until then, it was just me and my mama and daddy. We had a lot of good friends, and all of us went to fish fries and barbecues. I was seldom left home with a babysitter. All of our friends got together, and they all had kids. This way, the kids could also be a part. If it wasn't something the kids could go to, my parents didn't want to go.

A lot of our friends drank beer and stuff, but everything was all in fun for the kids. Once, at a fish fry, I asked, "What does that fish eye taste like?" We popped it out, fried it, and ate it—all in fun. Their attitude was, if something didn't hurt you, it was okay to do it as long as you were respectful.

My daddy was in the freight business. He was like a broker and represented several companies. My mom didn't work. She had everything she needed. But my mom was one of those people who never seem satisfied with anybody. The day she left, I remember she had one foot in the car and one foot out. Daddy and I were standing at the open screen door.

Mama asked, "Who you wanna live with?"

"I'm gonna stay with Daddy," I said.

She said, "Okay," and got in her car, and that was it.

My dad took up with his old high school sweetheart. She had three kids from a previous marriage. It was hard being a stepchild. It seemed like I got the blunt force of it all and always got the worst stuff to do. Now that I'm older and I talk to her kids, I realize the new "family" was hard on them too.

When I was seven or eight years old, I moved to Jackson, Mississippi, with my mama. She had a lot of marriages and a lot of boyfriends. One of them was very violent—not so much to me, but to Mama. I would try to interfere, to hit him with a baseball bat or something like that. He'd run off and be gone three days or so. Then he'd come back.

During those years, Mama and I didn't have anything. After she left Daddy, she worked, but she had only part of her high school education. She worked on the line at a couple of factories. Then she worked over at the fuel center of a truck stop and at a couple of department stores, just odds-and-ends stuff. I stayed by myself. I cooked and kept things picked up.

The two of us had a little Volkswagen beetle. It was so much fun! The faster we went, the louder the engine got, and the faster the windshield wipers swiped. When we turned a hard corner to the left, the right door would fly open. It was just awful! But Mama and I became close friends during that time.

We moved to Richland and lived in an apartment. I hated school there. I fought going, and I ditched school a lot. Mama called the law, and they came and got me several times. I never shoplifted or got into any other kind of trouble. I just didn't go to school.

Mama went through several relationships. I'd get close to one of her boyfriends and then he'd be gone. I started depending on myself. I built a wall around myself so I could not be hurt. I had no emotions at all. I was thirteen or fourteen at the time.

During this time, I'd visit Daddy, and the visit would be a holy war. It got to where I wouldn't go, which was fine with me. I was on the football team in Richland, and Daddy and his new family never came to a football game. They never came to see where we lived. They never came to my JROTC functions. Nothing.

I played center, and I was told I had a football scholarship waiting for me. I was also in JROTC, at least until I quit high school. I could have gone anywhere in the country with JROTC. I was a hefty kid, about six feet tall. From the time I could get a job, I worked construction or yard work or whatever, and those jobs made me strong.

I still wasn't doing schoolwork. I told the teachers, "Hey, look, I'm not gonna do your homework, but I'll make a deal with you. If I ace your test … you'll pass me."

They'd say, "There's no way you can ace that test."

Well, I aced the tests. That's how I got through most of the schools I went to. I got Cs. I could have made As and Bs, but Cs and Ds were where I was at. No one cared what grades I got. No one explained to me what the repercussions of bad grades would be.

Then Mom married a guy named Danny. He picked at my mom and set her nerves off, which was easy to do. He figured early on how to do it. One day, he grabbed Mama and threw her on the floor. It was unusual for him to go that far, and he shouldn't have done it at all. I came unglued and went after him. I was sixteen years old. I broke all the kitchen cabinets with him. I put him against the wall so hard that it broke the outside siding. I could have killed him, but I didn't.

That was the end of me living with them. I left, but I didn't have anywhere to go. Mama didn't know where I went. I stayed at different people's houses for a while and worked some construction jobs. I was a good laborer. Whatever it was, I could do it. I learned how to drive nails, cut boards, and make every step count.

In the meantime, Mama left Danny. She figured out where I was, and we moved back to the apartment complex we had lived at before Danny came along. By then her nerves were shot, and she checked herself into a mental facility. Once again I was alone. So I ditched school and went to work at a grocery store. I excelled there. I started out bagging groceries, and then I went to work in the produce department.

During my working hours, I did fine. After hours, I started drinking and shooting pool. Sometimes I'd stay out all night long, coon hunting. It got to the point where anyone who knew me saw me either drinking or going to get a drink. I also started smoking. I was a rough guy, but I kept my job because I was a good, strong worker with a friendly attitude. People told me my dark-haired looks weren't bad, either.

Or so a slim, pretty, fifteen-year-old girl told me not long after she came into the store looking for a gift …

I had just finished stacking up the five-pound bags of potatoes and was sweeping the linoleum when she came up to me. "I need to buy some flowers," she said.

"Who for?"

"My boyfriend," she answered.

"So, what's he getting you?"

"Prob'ly nothing," she said.

"Well, I'll send you something since it's Valentine's Day," I told her. "I'll make 'em real special and send 'em on over to your school." I recognized her as someone from the school I was supposed to be attending, but I didn't know her.

I kidded around with her and then forgot all about the conversation. The next day I went out to my truck, and it was filled up with balloons.

She came around the corner and said, "You never sent me anything!" We started talking, and it kind of escalated from there. Even though I wasn't attending high school, everybody from there liked me. I could go there and hang out, so I did. I'd pick her up from school and take her home or whatever. I was more popular than I ever knew. I wasn't a prep, and I wasn't thug, either, but everybody knew me.

I wanted to join the navy, like my best friend did after he graduated, so I talked to a recruiter. Since I had taken JROTC I thought I'd get in easy. I took the test. I think I got a fifty-one. Unfortunately, to get in without a high school diploma, I needed to score a sixty.

"That's stupid," I said. "My buddy got a thirty-five, and he got in."

"That's because he graduated," the recruiter told me. "Here's a book. Go study it and take the test in six months."

"In six months this urge will be gone," I said, as if I had anywhere to go.

Then Mama met another guy at a bar, another "Danny." She moved in with him. This one was cool to me. The only problem was that he drank—a lot.

Mama told him, "You gotta quit drinking," but he wouldn't. After all, they'd met in a bar, so expecting him to stop was really "out there." He wasn't mean. He was … well … just a drunk, a good ol' guy. We lived in Jackson with him, but I knew it wouldn't last. It had gotten to the point where I didn't even want to unpack my boxes. I didn't know where we were going to be next.

I didn't want to go anywhere. A'Leta and I were dating, and everything was going good between the two of us. I worked for A'Leta's daddy, Lemuel, doing "road boring," putting pipe under roads and railroads. I made good money, but it got to the point where instead of Lemuel hiring a full crew, it was just the two of us. I didn't know how to take it. We were working six days a week, every week, no matter what. He owned the company, and in his mind, he had to do it. I respected his work ethic and soon adopted it, but for a young man in love, it was too many hours.

I learned a lot. I probably learned more working for Lemuel than I did anywhere else, but I got sick of the long hours. I found a job with an elevator company, building elevator doors and taking care of all the parts. My cousin worked there as a journeyman, and he got me the job. He tried to get me into the union, but not soon enough. The company told me I was going to be laid off.

I put in an application at American Freight, but they were under a hiring freeze. I got unemployment—I hated that—and waited for American Freight. When American Freight called, I worked a few different jobs and then started what we called "hostlin'"—moving trailers from door to door. It's hard work, but I loved it. I got my CDL driver's license and started driving eighteen-wheelers, delivering freight. Business got slow and I had to quit doing that.

By now, I had rented a little one-bedroom apartment. I promise—it was little! It wasn't but about forty feet by forty feet. A'Leta helped me pick out a nice bed for it, which we still have today! She had graduated from high school and was attending community college, studying to be a medical assistant while also doing secretarial work at her daddy's business. She started taking care of most of my bills, even though we weren't married. When I lived in that little place, we had so much fun. I think it was the most fun we have ever had.

I was partying hard, but I started going to church with A'Leta. I'd been to church when I was a kid, but never anything major. A'Leta's family always went to church. At first, I went just so I could be with A'Leta. Then one day I realized I needed to get saved. I went to her mama and daddy and told them I needed to talk to the preacher.

Well, I did get saved—I asked Jesus to forgive my sins and come into my life. But I didn't have that overnight transformation that some people think is supposed to take place. It is often a process one must go through to change the habits that have developed. It takes time, and it was that way for me. I was twenty years old, and I was still partying. During our dating time, I would pick A'Leta up and then she'd have to drive us back to her house. Then I would pull across the street to the church parking lot, stare at that old cross on the building, then pass out.

I was never addicted to alcohol. I just wanted to have a good time! I couldn't have cared less about the high. I just enjoyed the taste, and the high was a plus. A'Leta never did drink or do anything risky. She was always the sane one.

After we dated for what seemed like twelve years but was really only two, we planned to get married. I gave her a little ring on Mother's Day. We decided to surprise everybody at a church picnic and get married there. We wanted everyone to be able to come and be comfortable in a casual, carefree atmosphere.

CHAPTER 4

MARRIAGE AND THE BIRTH OF AN ANGEL

A'Leta

I loved the way Jack had become part of our church and was going with me all the time. In fact, I insisted he went. He was still partying, but I could see changes in him little by little.

I called Jack and woke him up at his little apartment. "Why don't we get married on Saturday at the church picnic?"

"Okay," he answered. "Whatever." He hung up and went right back to sleep, I think.

Later that evening he called and asked, "Did I just tell you we're getting married on Saturday?"

"You did, Jack," I told him. I'm pretty sure he was surprised! But he went along with it.

We let my mama in on the plan, but no one else knew except our pastor, Brother Mal, the guy doing the cooking, and a few close friends. "Big Vern" and Ron Swaggart were going to cook chicken gizzards and livers—my favorite—for our wedding dinner. I'm a southern girl, after all!

We woke up early on Saturday morning to rain. It had rained all night, and it didn't look like it was going to stop any time soon. Brother Mal called and wanted to know if we were still getting married. I said, "Yeah, we're getting married *somewhere*."

"You can use the church fellowship hall," Brother Mal said. We made a few phone calls, and Mrs. Brenda, Mrs. Jackie, Mrs. Beverly, and a few others had the church beautifully decorated. Big Vern and Ron, two of the best cooks in Rank in County, went ahead with frying the chicken parts from the picnic. We had the ceremony in the church. No one knew we were getting married until two hours prior to the ceremony—but there were more than one hundred people there!

During the ceremony the power went out. We got married by candlelight on April 26, 1997. The ceremony was simple, but it was good. It turned out that our wedding was one of those that people talked about for years after the fact. It has been over fourteen years, and they're still talking about it.

Jack

I didn't get to taste even one chicken gizzard or liver!

A'Leta was beautiful walking down that aisle. My eyes worked their way down from the awesome dress she was wearing to her feet, and I saw no shoes. That was fine with me! Her beautiful feet were the second things I had noticed about her when we met. She is sexy from one end to the other.

She moved in with me in that little apartment, and the fun began. We later bought a little house in D'lo, Mississippi. We began talking about having kids, but I was afraid. I didn't want kids because of what I'd been through.

We had our rocky moments like anybody else, but we got through them. Something slowly changed inside me. I called her from work one day and said, "Hey, let's have a kid." The next day, she was pregnant. That's how fast it was. There wasn't any practicing. It was like *poof!* There she was, pregnant.

I was still working with American Freight, but things had slowed down. I was sitting by the phone every day to see if I could work. I started working for A'Leta's dad again, cleaning vent-a-hoods. A'Leta had also been working for her dad before she got pregnant. But I didn't want her to be around the chemicals we used, because of the baby.

I did have good benefits at American Freight, which had already been a huge blessing. Not long after we got married, A'Leta—bless her heart—would be in such pain she would scream in the middle of the night. It was her gallbladder. Thank God for good health insurance. Her pain got so bad at one point, I called her daddy and said, "Just come get her. I don't know what to do."

I finally made her go to the doctor. Lo and behold, her gallbladder was messed up.

A'Leta

I remember having bad pains back when I was as young as three or four. They were so bad that my mother took me to the doctor. He always said it was stress that caused the pain, or something like that. They never checked any further, yet my sisters Tamyra and Angela were always talking about my complexion. They called it "yellowy." I had been like that forever. We didn't know it was a symptom of anything more serious until the pain became unbearable and I had to have my gallbladder removed.

We got through it, and I was fine after that. Before long, I was pregnant.

Then we had Carney—Jacquelyn Carney, though we've always called her "Carney." Carney is a family name, my grandmother's middle name, and my great-grandmother's maiden name. She was born on July 29, 1999.

I went into labor and called Jack. My daddy and he were working. I said, "I think my water broke about three hours ago."

Jack said, "Whaddaya mean 'you think'?"

"Well, either it broke or I peed in the bed."

He said, "Have you called your mama or anybody?"

"No."

"Don't you think you need to call somebody? 'Cuz it's been a long time!"

The night before, our friends Jason and Allison were over. I remember saying, "I'm sick and tired of being pregnant."

Allison had heard castor oil would bring on labor (although it hadn't worked for her). I had already gotten some, so I drank it. Well, it must have worked!

Allison told me later she felt bad, because Carney came a couple weeks too early. She was only about five pounds. Her lungs weren't developed. I look back now and realize how insane Allison and I were back then. We were just a couple of southern, young, broke, crazy, married Mississippi girls having babies.

Jack

When A'Leta went to the hospital, I was out working with her dad. I told Lemuel, "Look, you gotta take me to the hospital."

"It's going to take two days for her to have that baby," he said.

"I don't care if it takes *twenty* days. I'm gonna be at the hospital."

He took me, and the doc said, "You got plenty of time. Go home, get your shower, get the car seat, all that."

I didn't like leaving her, but I went and cleaned up and got the things we needed at the hospital. She never complained. The nurses were saying, "Something isn't right."

A'Leta would be lying there, and she'd announce, "Here come the contractions."

Her mama had talked her into taking an epidural. Next thing we knew, A'Leta was asleep.

A'Leta

They had to wake me to start pushing! I said, "This is easy!"

Jack said, "Not for me!" He was a nervous wreck. He held his breath every time I pushed.

My mother hollered at him, "Jack, you gotta breathe!" Every time I pushed, he pushed. No matter what happens in our family, it's dramatic. We could have our own reality show! It would be hilarious, but I don't think the rest of the world could handle it.

Jack handed the baby to me. She was so little! A nurse demanded, "Give me that baby." She weighed her, pricked her foot, and did all that. Then she took her and left the room. That was the last we got to hold her for seven days, because they put her in the NICU. We never got a specific name for Carney's condition, but we were told the natural lubricant in her lungs was not there, so they had to put a tube in them and pump some in.

For me, it was like the end of the world. I didn't want to go home. It was one of the worst feelings I've ever had—going home and not taking our baby with us. It made me think about someone who loses a baby, how the mama has to go home with nothing to show for the rough hours, knowing her baby is not alive. It made me more able to relate to their pain. I was able to understand how those women feel, and I've never forgotten it.

My mother is very outspoken. It's not that she *wants* to hurt your feelings, but she doesn't think about whether what she is about to say is going to hurt your feelings before she says it. She said, "You gotta get up. You can't stay here at the hospital. You gotta go home."

"I can't go home!"

"This hotel is too expensive, and we are going home!" Mama won the battle that day, anyway.

We went back every day for seven days, for each feeding time. A lady at our church, Lola, one of the most godly women I've ever known, a nurse in the NICU, stayed right by Carney's side the nights she was working. We knew Lola would make sure our baby was taken care of. That was one of those times you look and realize God was in complete control.

Carney was eight days old when I finally got to hold her. We took her home wearing a big "space suit" because she had jaundice. I am not exaggerating when I say that her skin looked fluorescent yellow at first.

Jack was kind of "old school" on how to take care of babies. He did not have a clue, but he sure thought he did! I had learned early on to humor him. He'd say, "We've got to lay this baby on the floor by the window in the sun, and we have to take her outside to get some light." I thought putting her in the sun would give her UV light like the light we brought home from the hospital was supposed to do. And every time we put her in her crib, we made sure it was in the sun. Before long, the jaundice was gone.

A NEW JOB

Jack

I was still working in and out of town for A'Leta's dad, so I had to leave my wife and little baby by themselves soon after Carney was born.

With a wife and new baby, I knew I had to make enough money to support all three of us. It was more difficult than I ever imagined. I found a job working for the local water department. A'Leta had finished her degree at Hinds Community College and had her associates degree. She had also passed the test for Certified Medical Assistant. However, she needed to stay home with Carney, who was so little she had to be fed what seemed like all the time.

The doctor had told A'Leta that the only way he would not worry about Carney was if she breast fed her. A'Leta was determined. She had pumped for seven days while Carney was in ICU, but, as she says, "Your body knows that the pump is not your baby."

Her milk was okay, but there wasn't enough to pump *and* save so she could go to work. She quit working and stayed home with Carney. We had to supplement A'Leta's milk with formula because Carney was so little.

We decided to sell our house, but we had nowhere to go. A'Leta's daddy had bought a twelve-by-thirty-two-foot trailer for A'Leta's grandmother. We put it behind his house. I had the job with the water department, but I wasn't making enough to start building. We couldn't do a whole lot, so we stayed in that little trailer. We fixed it up, and it was great. I added a little room onto it, and we made that our bedroom. It was like living in the little one-bedroom apartment we had started out in.

Then I talked to my friend's dad, who worked in the oil field.

"Hmmm," I said, "I may be interested in that."

He said, "It's hard. It's nasty."

"I don't mind," I told him. "I don't know what the benefits are, but I need something to support my family."

A week and a half later I called him. "Hey, you heard anything about that job?"

"Are you serious?" he asked.

"Yeah, I'm serious as a heart attack. I think I'm ready."

He said, "Pack your bags. You're leaving Tuesday." It wasn't but a week away.

I gave notice to the water department and left for the oil rig. It was in southern Louisiana, just south of Baton Rouge, about three hours from where we lived.

I was on a land rig, working as a clean-up hand. Basically, I took out the garbage. I was just a gofer. Whatever they wanted me to do, I'd do. "Go fer this and go fer that." Cleaning and scrubbing, I didn't care. I was even picking up cigarettes. I was a "worm,"[1] a clean-up hand. That was in '02.

It was hard leaving at the beginning of each hitch week (a "hitch" is what we call the amount of time we spent away from home at work) to go down to Baton Rouge to work on the rig. Carney was almost three by this time. Sometimes I'd leave and look in the rearview mirror. She would be running down the road, chasing after me. It killed me to leave that child. She would keep up with me by phone when I was gone. I would call and ask her, "How much longer?" and she would say something like, "Four more days, Daddy."

A'Leta wasn't real happy about me being gone. She'd tell me that when I was away, everything fell apart. Something would need fixing, or a big problem would come up, and I wasn't there to deal with it. By this time she was working again, using her CMA certification.

But I was in the oil field, and I was working. I was doing whatever, rain or snow, it didn't matter. The rigs don't shut down for anything. I was working in New Roads, Louisiana, on Rig 72. A land rig might be a smaller operation than an ocean rig, but it's about the same kind of work, and it's easier to move to different locations. You can move a land rig with special eighteen-wheelers. You work twelve hours and then you're off for twelve hours. The company provides the guys with a crew trailer. There's a refrigerator, a microwave, beds—nothing fancy—just a place to sleep and eat.

It was all right for me. We had a lot of fun in that trailer. Most people in the oil fields are kin to one another. I didn't know anybody, so I had to make it on my own, make my own name. I had to prove I could do any job. The way I got started working on the floor was that I outworked a guy. That had always been my ethic—I wanted to be the best. I had gone up and watched the floor hands so I could learn how to do their jobs, and I started relieving them so they could take breaks. It got to the point where one guy wanted to take breaks all the time, so I just stayed on the floor. Finally, the driller said, "I want this guy on my crew. You take this other guy and let him be clean-up hand. Put Billy Jack on my crew."

So, I wasn't clean-up hand but for two hitches. Out there, it's a dog-eat-dog world. If you don't work, you don't stay. A lot of times, it doesn't have anything to do with your mama or daddy or whatever. If you don't work, you don't stay. There are no holidays. I got to where I wanted to learn other things. I wanted to learn other positions. I didn't want to stay a "worm." I wanted to learn every job, and I picked them up pretty fast.

The rig had drilled a few different holes in different locations. We then moved it to Wennie, Texas. A hand named Bennie Earl and I rode together at this time to save money. He was our derrick man, and he and I became pretty tight. He taught me anything I wanted to learn. I asked my driller at the time, Lamar, if I could go up there with Bennie Earl, and he said, "Get it, boy." I wasn't there five minutes and ol' Bennie Earl hollered as he was going down the ladder, "See ya at crew change."

Then Rig 72 stacked in a pasture in southeast Texas (there was no more work to do on that rig). The contracts ran out, and companies like Shell, Marathon, or BP chose not to rent the rig. That meant there was no more work lined up for that rig. The tool pusher does all he can to find the best hands jobs on other rigs within the company. I must have impressed our tool pusher, Jerry, because he found me a job on Rig 226.

A'Leta and I had started building our new house, so I was working both places—on the rig and at home. I wanted to provide for my family while I was young so we could prepare for the future. So began my weekly trips from our little trailer in Florence, Mississippi, back to New Roads, Louisiana, to work on Rig 226.

I knew working on a rig had its hazards, but the company I worked for and the company the rig worked for were serious about safety. I had made it up to working motors on Rig 72, but since our rig had stacked, the only position on the new rig was back in the worm corner. I was just happy to have a job!

Soon, I started working derricks for a guy they had moved up; he was scared of heights. It was over a hundred feet in the air! It wasn't long before I had the job. My driller had been the assistant driller on Rig 72, so we had already built up a lot of mutual trust and worked well together. That's a must, and we had it. Plus, I was young, I was strong, and I was serious about my job. I wanted to learn everything I could, and I took care of my business. I didn't expect people to do my job. We were all serious about safety. I'd be careful, and I'd be okay.

On March 3, 2006, Rig 226 was working for a company in Nacogdoches, Texas. I usually arrived at the rig about an hour before my twelve-hour tour started. We were going to be "tripping pipe,"[2] taking pipe out or putting it into the hole, which is very hard work. The company didn't want to make the mud weight heavy enough to keep the gas down so it couldn't escape, which is called underbalanced drilling. It's a way to save money and time … if it works.

I knew this, and yes, it is a little more dangerous, but we thought we had put all the needed pieces in place. The contracting company did put into place the things that were understood to keep us safe. The mud weight rate needed to be increased, but a rotating head "RCD" (rotating control device) is designed to drill under pressure. It was our understanding that it was good up to 2500 pounds of pressure. In fact, "2500" was part of its designation. It has a huge, cone-shaped rubber that allows you to move the pipe under pressure, while allowing pressure to escape through the flow line.

On March 3, 2006, there was about 950–1050 psi on the "stripper rubber," which is the most important part of the RCD. I was standing up on the derrick board with about two and a half rows of pipe, about ninety feet above the rig floor and the rest of the crew. Mud weight and viscosity needed to be increased—the pressure had been at about 400–600 pounds, well below the supposed safety factor on the RCD, which was understood to be 2500 pounds. The stripper rubber[3] was practically brand-new.

Our crew was great at what we did, and we all looked out for each other. I felt pretty safe working around these guys. It was my family away from home. I knew that if anything bad happened, those guys knew what to do. A'Leta already knew who to call—my cousin Chris. "Chris'll handle everything," I had told her.

Little did I know that A'Leta would soon need to call him regarding a situation that would be worse than anyone could have ever imagined.

FROM DADDY'S GIRL TO BILLY JACK'S GIRL

A'Leta

My family was about as different from Billy's as they could be. My parents, Lemuel and Edra Combs, were married young. My great-grandparents were the McMillians, a prominent family in a small town in Arkansas. They owned rental property, a service station, and some other things. My parents have been married for forty years, and I never heard the word "divorce" used seriously around my family. I hardly even knew what the word meant. In many ways, I was very sheltered.

I am the third of four children. Tamyra is sixteen years older than me, Angela is ten years older, and our brother, Lemuel Austin Combs II (who we call "Tu"), is six years younger than me. That's a big spread in years between us, but we're all close.

I have an unusual name. It's made from "Angela, Lemuel, Edra, and Tamyra." My sister Tamyra came up with the idea of adding the apostrophe to make the name more exotic and unique, and their new baby sister became "A'Leta." She succeeded in that, all right. I have been made fun of and complimented on my name, and it is almost always mispronounced.

I was born in DeWitt, Arkansas, but when I was in third grade, my daddy bought the construction company he worked for. He did very well for himself, and we didn't hurt for anything because my parents always thought of us kids. My daddy is retired now, and he and my mom spend a lot of time with us. My brother, Tu, recently bought my dad's business.

My mother was—and still is—very outspoken and was a strict disciplinarian. We weren't abused, but we kids were whipped back into shape whenever she thought we needed it. Today I thank God for that, or we all might have ended up in jail.

There is something a little quirky about my family. I can see it now that I'm grown up. Some of us have a tendency toward "ADHD" (attention deficit hyperactivity disorder), myself included. Carney too. She needs a lot of structure. We are not perfect parents, but we are pretty strict with her, though not like my mother was. Carney is sassy and lacks self-control in what she says. I think she's a lot like me!

But back to how I was raised. Our Baptist church was very important to our family. My grandmother, Gertrude Carney Farish McMillian, was a godly woman, and her influence on me was strong. I was saved, as they call it in the South and other places when you accept Christ as your personal Savior, when I was only six. Our pastor, Riley Pool, at East side Baptist Church was one the most godly men I have ever known, and he baptized me. We loved that man. He died recently at the age of eighty-one.

During my high school years I worked for my daddy. I was fifteen—our work ethic is something Jack and I have in common. I still went to church, though I didn't really know what a close relationship with Christ was all about. I wouldn't understand that until I was twenty-seven years old. My parents recognized the gift of mercy in me early on. Even as a child, I was always helping my friends with something or other. Now, I also know I have the gift of mercy. I seem to be attracted to needy people. Over the years, those spiritual gifts sometimes change as a person's relationship with God changes and matures, but this one's always been part of me.

I started dating when I was fifteen. I had a few other boyfriends for a short time, but never anyone serious until I started dating Billy Jack. "Jack" (or "Big Sexy" as I always called him), was not my parents' first choice for their baby girl. He was just another redneck dropout in their eyes. But right from the start Jack was very romantic. He was always sending me flowers and taking me on dates that required a lot of creativity. I am not exaggerating when I say our romance was the "fairy tale" romance every girl dreams about.

Jack would take me on wonderful dates and then party afterward. My convictions prompted me to put a stop to that "or else." He accepted Christ and began trying to learn and grow as a new Christian. There were times when he reverted back to his old ways, but I understood the reason. It's easy to do when all you've known is pool halls and you love the taste of alcohol.

We were young, dumb, and in love, so we had our share of drama. We had tons of fun, bruised egos, and a few too many tears. Despite all that, we eventually kissed and made up. My daddy has always said that fighting is worth it because there's nothing more fun than making up. That was true of us! Neither of us has ever strayed from the other. We have had our share of issues, but we have always worked through them. Truth is, Jack was my everything.

That sounds good, but it is a flawed attitude. There was one problem with our fairy-tale romance. Jack was supposed to be my perfect husband, never disappointing me and always knowing exactly what I was thinking—even when I was too stubborn to look at him, much less speak to him. As a man, Jack was not able to give me perfect love that would never fail. He was not capable of always keeping Carney and me safe. He could not promise he could always provide for our needs.

I wouldn't realize that only God could be all the things for me that I expected Jack to be until God was the only One I could turn to.

"I'M A DEAD MAN"

Jack

The fire was intense, and it was burning me alive! In seconds, I had become a dead man. I figured I was dead either way: burned, still burning, and in long, drawn-out agony, or broken by a fall and quickly put out of my misery by hitting the ground.

The paint and the rope on the derrick were still burning. My nylon harness was melting into me, and my skin was sloughing off. I knew I was a dead man. The ends of my fingers exploded, and bodily fluids poured out like water from a hose. I tried to jump into the flames. I was dead, anyway—I might as well make it quick. I landed on my back on the derrick board.

While the rams were closing the hole off, the fire got more intense and the pressure got worse. It was like putting a finger over a water hose, and the water shoots farther. This was the same way, but with fire. Just before the fire went out, I looked down. My penis looked like a candle. My clothes were incinerated. Only my boots were still on. I kept beating myself, trying to put out the fire, but I just sloughed off skin and muscle. Bodily fluids poured out from my raw, exposed body.

The fire was like a fuse, burning the paint on the derrick legs from bottom to top. The grease and rope we use to hold the pipe coming out of the derrick was still burning. As the last flame went out, I made it to the ladder. I planned to jump into the back of the parts bin. It was full of one inch pegs, pup joints, and valves. I knew the fall would kill me. I wanted to die—I *needed* to die.

Moments before I could fall from the derrick, my driller, Billy Humble, appeared on the board. Later they told me Billy was climbing up to me at a rate of about four to six rungs per step, straight up. That's impossible! But they saw it. It looked like someone was pulling him up by the collar.

If Billy had been drilling, if he'd been sitting at the chair, there's no way I could have survived. It would have taken an extra second or more for him to hit those buttons. But since he was standing there behind the assistant driller, he was able to hit them fast. He had a green something—a large cloth—in his hands. The back of my neck—down both shoulders—was still on fire. He wrapped the green cloth around me and put out my smoldering body.

"Billy, take care of my wife and Carney," I told him.

"I will, buddy," he said.

"Good, I'm fixin' to jump."

"No, Jack, I can't let you do that."

"You can't stop me."

"No, Jack, don't do that."

"Billy, I don't wanna live like this. Look at me! I'm burned up, man."

Now, Billy Humble liked to drink his beer and have a good time. He wasn't a religious person, but he said, "Let's pray." If Billy Humble wanted to pray, I knew I was in really bad shape! He prayed the best he knew how. Even now, I think it's the sweetest thing I have ever heard in my life.

When he got through, he said, "Come 'ere, lemme hold you. I wanna hold you, Jack."

"Billy, you can't. You can't." Whatever he touched would slough off or break off. The tips of my fingers were pouring liquid; bits and pieces of skin and flesh were flying everywhere. "Billy, don't touch me," I said. "If I start to fall, don't try to grab me."

During those few minutes, I went from wanting to die one second to wanting to live the next second. From screaming and cussing one minute to praying and crying the next minute.

By this time, Hossie, the assistant driller, had made it up there in just seconds. Now, these are strong men, but most of the time, you have to stop somewhere halfway up to catch your breath when you're climbing without assistance. These two guys were hands-on ready, never stopped, and amazingly didn't seem out of breath.

"Come 'ere, Jack, I'll tote you down," Billy told me.

"Hell, Billy," I said. "You can't, bud. Who's watching the well? What's the pressure on the well, Billy?"

"I don't know," he admitted.

"Billy, somebody's got to look at the pressure on the well," I said.

Right now, I was the only one seriously hurt. But if this thing blew again, everybody would be dead because everybody was trying to get up here to me. Two of the men, Shakey and Richard, were on the rig floor when the well blew. They slid down the handrails on their arms and got the underside of their arms burned from sliding. The backs of most of the guys' necks got a little blistered from the heat. When Shakey hit the ground, he turned to the right. The floor mats—about an inch and a half thick, solid, heavy rubber with steel spikes so you can get traction on the floor when it gets slick—were falling all around him. He heard *boom, boom*, everywhere.

Shakey is an awesome guy and had the reflexes of a cat. His philosophy was, if it goes *boom*, RUN! It doesn't matter what it is. You run first and see what's left afterwards. He ran and dove underneath the company man's trailer and came out the other side. He told me later that as soon as he came out from under the trailer, he thought about me. He looked up, and I was screaming. It was the awfullest thing he'd ever seen and heard in his life. He said, "You were one-hundred percent on fire."

But back to Billy and Hossie being there with me on the board …

Billy asked, "Can you climb down?"

"Look at my hands, man." I could see the bones and ligaments. The skin was gone. "I can't. You're gonna have to go get that work basket."

The work basket was something we never used—well, until those few seconds. It was way off on the back side of the location, behind everything in the world. Billy hollered down at Shakey, "Go get the basket!"

I watched Shakey run and jump onto the fork lift seat, put it in high gear, and scoot across location to get the basket. He brought it to the rig's V-door. The hands rigged it up and brought it to the rig floor. He didn't even remove the test weight on the bottom—that's how big a rush he was in. It seemed like this took a long time, but it was probably only a few minutes. The gang "elected" Tad to get in the basket to come and help me.

The basket was about four feet by four feet square, big enough to hold both of us. When Tad got closer to me, his eyes teared up and grew large. I knew he couldn't help it. He's a soft-spoken guy, and I could see on his face that it just killed him to know what he had to do. As they brought the basket up, it got wedged between the cable that held the block and the derrick board. They couldn't get it up to me. I had to climb down into the basket. Tad tried to help, but when he saw me, he froze. There wasn't much he could do.

No wonder. You couldn't touch me. You couldn't pull on me. You couldn't do any of that. Where could he even get a grip on me? I was oozing, dripping blood and water. Skin and muscle were flying off what was left.

I climbed down into that basket by myself. As I climbed in, I leaned up against the side, looked at Tad, and said, "I'm sorry." I didn't want anyone to be hurt because of me. There was only one thing on my mind, and it was the crew. I kept asking how everyone was, who was hurt and how bad. Tad assured me everybody was all right.

We didn't say anything to each other all the way down. I was screaming. Screams of pain beyond describing, screams of a man condemned, screams that must have been horrible to hear. Some of the screams were prayers: "God, help me!" "Take me, Lord!" "Let me die now!" Others were probably untranslatable, and others would probably be unprintable, words even I didn't know I knew.

We got about halfway down, and I saw Shakey. I'd always told Shakey that if the rig blew out or whatever, to get me down—don't leave me. He was already feeling like crap because he had left me. I got halfway down and hollered, "Shakey? Shakey!"

The look on his face was like he had seen a monster. My clothes were gone, and I could see what my body looked like. It was white, like charcoal looks before it flames up in a barbecue grill or like chicken when it hits the hot grate. People think that you turn black when you get burned. You don't. You turn bright white. You start turning black as the tissue dies.

Before I got in the basket, I thought my long johns had melted to me. I reached down and pulled them off. But the long johns were in reality pieces of skin.

That's when I knew, *really* knew. As I came down, blood, fluids, meat, skin, and body parts were falling. They were everywhere. The rig floor looked like a murder scene from a movie.

We got down to the floor. If you go to most construction sites, they have this little chicken-wire-type gurney made out of metal. It's light but strong. If you lie down in it, you can be carried down if you're injured. The men had tried to line it the best they could with their jackets and their shirts. Guys were standing around in the cold with no shirts on. Even a number of the third-party hands who had been in trailers were out there just in their boots and underwear, trying to help. One of them—I can't remember his name but I'll never forget him—was a real sweet guy. He worked for the "MWD" hands, which stands for "measure while drilling."[4]

Shakey opened the door. I walked out of the basket, and the guys picked me up. "Don't you drop me!" I told them. Adron "Bulldog" Brown, my tool pusher,[5] was standing right there to my left. Shakey was at my head. The MWD hand was on the other side, and Billy Humble and Hossie were at my feet.

I could see in their eyes that I was dead. They were trying to console me. One minute I'd cuss and scream; the next minute I'd pray. One minute I wanted to die; the next minute I wanted to live. I looked up at Bulldog. We had always had a good relationship—I'd cuss him out some days, and some days he'd cuss me out, but that's the way it was out there. If you had something you needed to say, you just said it. I looked at Bulldog and begged him, "Please, please don't let me die."

He looked at me and said, “You ain’t gonna die on my hitch, son.”

They got me down the steps and laid me in the gurney on the ground. I was on the men’s jackets for the most part. Someone asked, “Well, how we gonna get him out of that and onto the ambulance gurney?”

I was short-tempered, so I pulled myself up and walked over to the ambulance and laid down on the ambulance gurney. I was a dead man, but somehow I was able to walk. I heard someone say, “Go ahead, He-man!”

But I knew human power had nothing to do with me being able to walk.

CHAPTER 8

DEAD MAN BREATHING

Jack

"Sorry—I don't have nothin' left on but my boots," I mumbled.

My privates were out in the open. They were burned. I knew they looked bad, but I had to carry on. A nurse sat at my left inside the ambulance. She had her cell phone. "Call my wife and tell her I love her. And will you have her tell Carney that her daddy loves her so much?" They don't usually call, but she did this time.

Most EMTs, fire workers, and other emergency crews might go their whole career and never see anybody burned like I was and still be alive. They were in panic mode. They acted like they didn't know what to do. I was a volunteer fireman, and I knew the shape I was in. I'd been through EMT training. I knew I was bad-off.

I had seen people in a car wreck who had burned to death. I looked just like them—except I was breathing. Up on the board, I had told Billy Humble I didn't want to live like this. He had said, "Billy Jack, you ain't that bad."

I asked him, "Do I still got my ears, my nose, my lips?"

He answered me, "Yeah. You ain't that bad."

Well, I *was* that bad. I lay there with the paramedic at my head, some EMTs at my feet, and the nurse at my side, and they began cutting my boots off.

"Whoa! Hold it! Don't cut my work boots off! Those boots are brand new! I'm gonna need them boots!" I began kicking and yelling, "Don't cut my &@^! boots off!"

I could feel my chest swelling up. I couldn't catch my breath, but I was surprised I'd lasted as long as I had. I reached up and grabbed the paramedic by his shirt. My hands were horrible-looking. "You gotta trache me."

"Man, I can't."

"You gotta trache me," I croaked.

He said, "Listen. Right now I gotta find a vein."

I sounded like a rough knife cutting through cardboard. "What vein? If you don't trache me, you're not gonna need a &@^! vein."

The guys at my feet were poking needles everywhere. Wherever they poked, there was nothing. I weighed about 235 pounds, and most of that weight was muscle. During the argument about the trache process, we hit a bump, and the EMT announced, "We're pulling into the hospital right now."

That's the last thing I remember. One of the emergency personnel told us later that the doctor who came down to trache me on arrival said, "I'm not gonna trache him," when he saw me. "He's gonna die, anyway."

A respiratory therapist insisted, "You're not doing your job. You're gonna trache him or you're gonna have to answer to me why you didn't. He was alive when he got here, and by God, you need to do everything you can to keep him alive." The doctor really had no choice.

I talked to him much later. He tried to justify what he had said. "You were dead. There was no reason for me to waste my time and the material to trache you."

In his defense, I'll say I had already swelled up. I'm sure I looked like I should be dead. I'm also sure he had never seen anyone in a condition as bad as I was. People can go through their whole careers and never see anybody like me. Most of the medical books had taught him not to trache me, to let me die. That's what's so unique about this. It goes against the medical and scientific teachings. It's a *miracle!*

Just before they put me into the helicopter, they asked Bulldog if he wanted to say anything before I left. I found out they completely shut down the rig location. Tad was sent to the end of the rig road and told not to let anyone in. Kenny Allen showed up for his tour that morning and immediately knew something was wrong. Tad told him, "I can't let you on location."

"What happened and who's hurt?" Kenny asked.

Tad was not supposed to tell him anything, but Kenny and I were close. We'd worked together a few years before he started drilling. We knew each others' families. I think Kenny told Tad he would kick his @*$ if he didn't tell him. So, he did, and Kenny drove around and flew down to the rig to see how bad it was. Those hands were on lockdown and could not leave location. On Sunday, they gave the company a choice: "Fire us or not, but we're going to the hospital to see Billy Jack."

A'Leta will explain what happened during the next several hours. It would be a couple of weeks before I would feel alive enough to realize I actually *was* alive.

THEY KNEW HE WASN'T GONNA MAKE IT

A'Leta

It was awhile before I could see Jack. By that time, his mom and her husband had arrived, and our good friends Shelley and Stephen were there. I don't remember Jack's dad being there yet—I think he was still on his way. I'm not sure if my sister Tamyra was there yet, though I do remember her being there soon after.

It was several hours before I went back to see Jack. I found out later why it took so long. When Dr. Sittig told me they were bandaging him up—"they're finishing bandaging him" was what he said—I didn't know "finishing" meant it would take them three hours. I didn't know until later how complicated bandaging him was, and that it would become a regular, painful, and time-consuming part of Jack's routine. Later, one of the nurses told me they would wrap him, but before they could get to the other end of his body, what they had just done was soaking wet from the fluids oozing out of his body. They had to wrap … and wrap … and wrap.

They did what Dr. Sittig had told them to do, but they were clearly thinking, *We're doing all this for nothing, because it is not possible for*

Billy Jack to live. However, burn nurses are very compassionate.[6] They must be special to do that job. They are not there if they don't want to be, because there are plenty of other nursing jobs. So they kept wrapping and kept wrapping.

Mr. Bob was pacing the floor. I said to him, "That tile's gonna have to be replaced by the time we get out of here." Watching him made me agitated. "Can someone go find out what's taking so long?" I begged to whoever was beside me. "Even if it's just to find out why it's taking a lot longer than they expected." Finally, we got to go back.

Since my education was in the medical field, I felt pretty knowledgeable about some things, and what was happening during those hours didn't add up. Normally, you wash your hands and gown up—head to toe—to keep from transferring any infections to the patient. We didn't have to wash our hands or gown up, or anything. Then I figured out why. It was not going to matter. Jack was not going to live. They were letting whoever wanted to see him to come in, because he was dying.

We went into the room—Bob, Shelley, Stephen, me, and Jack's stepdad at the time. His mom didn't go in because I wouldn't let her. She was squalling quite a bit, and I told her husband she couldn't go in to see Jack until she was ready to handle it.

"There will be no cryin' in that room," I said. "There will be no nothin'. There better not be a whimper, 'cause regardless of how much medicine he has, he can sense when somebody is upset, when somebody is hurting. He's not gonna have that worry and hurt on top of what he already has. Until you can get it together and know and handle the fact of what you're about to see, and take it, and get out, you are not going in." That rule applied to anyone visiting him, including myself. So, Jack's mom did not go in.

Jack was in a small room—partitioned only by curtains—right next to the nurse's desk in the burn unit. At first, the significance of where he was (not checked into a regular room) didn't register with me.

I went up to Jack and talked to him. Then I buried my head in Bob's chest and cried, but I hid the crying and didn't let Jack hear me. I talked to him, and he knew I was there. Every time he heard my voice, his heart rate went up on the monitor. So he knew I was there. He could hear me.

It is impossible to describe how swollen he looked. The IVs pumped in extra liquids to compensate for all of the bodily fluids he was losing. He looked like he weighed seven hundred pounds at least. The swelling was enormous; we couldn't even see his bed. He was bandaged up so heavily that only his eyeballs, his nose, and his mouth showed—just a little circle on his face. What little part of his face that was showing was black. Everything else was gauzed. His tongue was swollen and hung out of his mouth. He couldn't put it back in.

My Jack did not look human.

We stood there for as long as they let us, looking at someone none of us could recognize. We were actually in the hallway, and my mind didn't recognize the obvious: They hadn't put Jack in a "real" room because he wasn't going to be their patient for long. His hours on earth were winding down. No sense having to clean and prep a room after he died.

The night passed. In the morning, Jack was still alive—no one knew how or why he hadn't died. As my sister Tamyra and I opened the door to the burn unit that morning, we heard a horrendous crash. It sounded like the entire burn unit was coming down. Tamyra and I looked at each other. I could tell we were both thinking, *What the heck are they doing in there?*

We went around the corner to Jack's bed, still out in the middle of the hallway. His leg was hitting the tip of the bed. I thought, *No, I didn't really see that.*

The day nurse, a terrific young woman by the name of Terri, asked me, "Did you hear your husband?"

I said, "What, that crash?"

"Yeah."

"We heard it, but we didn't think anything about it because we knew it wasn't him," I told her.

"Oh, but it *was* him." Terri explained that he had figured out that in order to get her attention when he needed pain meds, he picked both legs straight off the bed and then slammed them down. "He's not even supposed to be alive!" she said. "He's not supposed to be moving. How he's doing that, I don't know!"

"Well, that's Jack," I told her. "Jack's a fighter, first of all. If anybody can survive this, it's Jack." I knew without a doubt that God was showing me he was going to deliver Jack.

The nurse was a short, petite thing. The next morning when she did his bandage change, she had to stop and set him straight. "This morning at dressing change," she told me later, "I had to have a little discussion with Jack because he was fighting me. I had to explain to him that he was a heck of a lot bigger than I was and I couldn't fight him. If he would just calm down and let me do this, I could get it done quicker and get it over with, and I wouldn't have to call another nurse to hold him down. After I talked to him, he stopped and calmed down, and he was fine."

"He probably wanted to know what you were doing," I said. "He likes to know everything that's going on. He's nosy. His normal nature is to know everything. Plus, the pain, I'm sure … I mean … there's not enough pain medicine. You can't ever give him enough."

From those very first hours, there were times when the pain was bad. Jack fought and tried to scream, but he had a tracheostomy.[7] We could hear nothing, and we couldn't do anything for him. It was so hard to watch! I was with him through many of those times, and I had to sit there, knowing I couldn't do anything.

The nurses soon got to know me and were on the prowl for me. I had to be there to calm Jack down and keep him from driving everybody around him insane. He was already out of his mind for obvious reasons of trauma, pain, and medications. They had to tie him to his bed because he would fight and be so anxious. But he didn't do that when I was there.

The nurses did not like tying Jack to his bed. It was no fun for a big boy like Jack to be out of control and helpless, and being tied up was incredibly painful on his peeled, tender, bandaged body. They used sheets and loosely wrapped them around his arms and to the bed so he couldn't get out. He signaled as well as he could that he was frantic for medicine to stop the horrific pain ravaging his body from head to toe.

"You have so many minutes left, and you can have your next dose," the nurses said. Then they would tell me, "It's not time for his meds yet," or "He can only have so much or there's the risk of causing death."

That didn't cut it, and it wasn't long before I was demanding, "I don't care if it's more than he can have. I don't care if it's everything the hospital has in their possession. Just give it to him."

The nurse on duty argued, "We can only give him so much so that we don't kill him."

"I don't care," I answered. I was desperate to give Jack some relief. "I'll sign something saying that I will not sue you because you overdosed him on pain medicine. I don't want him to suffer like that."

As the staff got used to Jack, they learned how far they could go with his pain medicine. However, during those first few hours and days it seemed like nothing could take away his pain. Dr. Sittig put him in an induced coma for a couple of weeks because of the pain, the many surgeries he was having, and so he could get some rest.

CHAPTER 10
CARNEY

A'Leta

Carney was six years old. She went to bed one night with her mama at home and her daddy away at work on the rig as usual. She woke up the next morning to learn that her daddy was dead (or would be soon, in the minds of everyone we knew), and her mama was gone.

She didn't know for a week that her daddy was hurt and still alive. My daddy came and picked her up out of bed and put her in the car with him the night Mr. Bob showed up at our front door. Daddy carried her out to his car. I saw her little head pop up for a second, but I didn't want her to wake up. I didn't want her to know that anything was going on. I didn't want to say, "Your dad's hurt and he's fine," and then have to tell her the next day he had died.

News about the explosion was all over the papers. Churches were praying for Jack, and everyone in town knew about it. Mother kept Carney out of school that week. She didn't even want to take her to the grocery store because she didn't want someone to say something about it.

That whole week Carney never asked, "Where's my mama?" She didn't ask, "Why is my daddy not home?"

My mom finally told her, "Carney, I don't want you to be scared to ask me. Do you want to know where your mom and daddy are, or are you wondering?"

Carney answered, "No, I know where they are."

"Where are they?" Mama asked her.

"My daddy came home from the rig and picked my mama up," Carney said. "He took her to the rig with him. They'll be back in seven days." No wonder Carney wasn't worried. God had taken all fear she might have had away from her. She made up this nice little story by way of explaining why she was with Nana.[8]

A week after Jack was taken to the hospital, Mama brought Carney to be with me for a while. I met them in the waiting area. Carney asked me, "Is this a hospital?"

"Yes it is, baby," I said.

"My daddy got hurt, didn't he?"

"He did," I said.

"I've gotta see him right now."

"They won't let you go in right now," I told her. "He's in ICU, and they won't let kids go back there."

"Mama! I've got to see him!"

"You'll have to wait, baby."

"How bad is it?"

"It's very bad. It'll be a long time, but Daddy will get better. He'll come home, but it'll be a very long time."

Carney wanted to see her daddy for herself. Not that she thought I was lying to her, but I think she just wanted to see for herself that he was alive. "You know, Mama," she said, "we're supposed to be really happy when people die."

I didn't understand what she meant at first. "We are?" I asked. "Why do you think that?"

"They go home to be with Jesus, so we're supposed to be happy."

I thought, *She's got a better understanding than any adult.* I'd had visions for probably eighteen months before the explosion that Jack would get hurt somehow. I wondered if Carney had also had dreams or visions but we hadn't known about them.

Carney has always been perceptive. She looked at me and said, "He's burnt."

She knew.

"PUT OUT THE FIRE!"—TRUTH AND FANTASY

Jack

"I'm on fire! Put out the fire! Put out the fire!"

When I came out of the coma, I woke up and started screaming. At least, I *tried* to scream, but having an intubation tube in my throat made it impossible to get anything more than a choking sound out. I didn't know it at first, but a week had passed with me in an induced coma. I had been burned on a Friday. It had taken a day or two to work myself off the bed—bandages, tubes out of both ends of my body, and everything else—onto the floor. I'm not sure how I did it. When it happened twice, Dr. Sittig put me in the coma that kept me out for a week.

A nurse appeared. "Mr. McDaniel, you're okay."

"Put out the fire! Please, put it out!"

Someone convinced me I wasn't on fire anymore.

The nurse told me I was at LSU Hospital in Shreveport, Louisiana. Then I think she hit the pain meds button, and I went back out. But not for long. I kept going through the fire again … and again. The flashbacks were some of the worst pain. They literally patted me down to convince me I was not on fire in my mind. I had always been told that crazy people had flashbacks. Let me tell you something! They are as real as the event itself.

I developed "ICU psychosis," a condition that's not uncommon. When you're in ICU, it's hard to know if it's day or night. You lose track of time, and you don't know where you are when you're heavily medicated. It is difficult for your body to know when to sleep and when not to. There were days without sleep, and that's when it gets dangerous.

They told A'Leta she could bring in some beer to see if that would get me to sleep. When that didn't work, she sneaked in some whiskey. Nothing helped. The only thing that calmed me down was A'Leta—something about her voice. I guess she was the only constant I had. Again, she is amazing. The visiting hours didn't apply to us. There were times when they'd have to bring A'Leta in right after surgery to get me to lie still and to quit fighting. They put a CD player in my room so I could listen to gospel and country music. Most music has a calming effect on people.

I was awake, but that was not a good thing, My mind continued to play tricks on me. I could still feel the fire burning off my clothes and my skin. I went through the fire again and again. Worse, I woke up from one surgery and couldn't see. The surgeon had sewn my eyes shut to keep them from constricting. I didn't know if I'd ever see again or not. My mind had to overcome the reality of my eyes not being able to open. I was in complete darkness. I couldn't talk or move. All I could do is listen.

I began to understand a little about darkness in the Bible and about the blind being made to see. I began to get a picture in my mind of what it was like to walk blind. Try this, and you'll get an idea of what I'm talking about: Open your eyes and then close them. You'll have an image in your mind of what you just saw. Now, keep them closed for a while. That image disappears with nothing to replace it. It's total darkness. That was the darkest place I had ever been—and I don't just mean in the bodily sense. I've been in the middle of some dark woods when hunting, but this was so much darker than that. The Bible says

God will lead the blind down unfamiliar paths. Well, I was certainly going down a path I didn't know.

I could barely communicate because of the tracheostomy, which I wanted like heck to rip out. I had a feeding tube down my nose, and I hated that too. I pulled at it and pushed it with my tongue. A'Leta was the only one who could understand and figure out what I needed. How she did this is still amazing to me, but she could read my lips. Normally, it takes years for someone to learn that. I would sometimes put my pretend cell phone to my mouth and "talk" to people. I imagined lots of things.

At one point after I was able to open my eyes a little, I was convinced A'Leta was having an affair. I lay in bed and looked down the hall. I could see her with him! The nurses and staff kept telling me, "You need to quit. You need to quit accusing her, because she's doing all she can." In my mind, it was real. I cussed her several times, but I was out of my mind and she knew it. But it had to be hard. I was on so much medicine. How she put up with that I'll never know.[9]

Dr. James Levinson, M.D., Vice-Chairman of the Department of Psychiatry at Virginia Commonwealth University Medical Center in *Psychiatry Weekly* online writes about a burn survivor's unique psychiatric issues:

> Delirium during the acute care of severely burned patients is very common, related to rapid, massive fluid shifts and electrolyte imbalance, hypoxia from smoke inhalation or shock lung, sepsis, medication side effects, and other organic factors ... it is very difficult to determine how much of a burn patient's agitation is due to delirium versus pain versus acute anxiety, especially since most patients will have all three to varying degrees during hospitalization in the burn unit.[10]

I was only twenty-eight years old, and I was going through all these hells, with no end in sight. I missed my wife so much! I wanted to feel her and smell her. The dead tissue up my nose stank so badly. A'Leta would sit and pull that crap out and oh! It stank! I'll just come out and say it. I missed sleeping with my wife. More than once I tried to convince a nurse to have sex with me. "Come on, honey, let's do it right now." I struggled to get the words out, and I bet it sounded like I was being strangled, but I could tell she knew what I was trying to say.

I don't know how those poor nurses put up with me. They must have been used to patients saying outrageous things like that. Like Mrs. Debbie, bless her heart, I asked her on the way back from surgery. She just pushed me into my room, laughed, and said, "Boy, you crazy."

During these few weeks, I was so trussed up, tied up, and wrapped up that I couldn't do anything on my own. Besides the intubation tube and a urine catheter, which remained in place for weeks, I had several IVs in different places in my arms. I also had a rectal tube, which had been put in place to keep my feces from getting on my body. It prevented infection and was supposed to stop some of the pain of relieving myself as soon as I could eat anything. It consisted of a tube with a small balloon at the end of the tube to collect the waste. The balloon enlarges the canal for the waste.

I remember one time when they came in to change out the tube. I felt them tugging on it, but it wasn't moving. I heard them say, "It's not deflating." They came over and said, "Mr. McDaniel, we have a problem. The balloon will not deflate, so you're going to have to tough it out."

I shook my head—as if I had a choice! I decided that when they pulled—since they were going to be down there—I was gonna push as if I was having a baby. I knew that waste was going to follow.

They got under the sheet and held my legs as if they were in stirrups. "Okay, Mr. McDaniel, here we go. *Do not push*!"

When that tube came out, I let 'em have it! It was like a scatter gun, and those interns looked like rats running from a cat. Hey, you've got to find *something* to make you laugh. From then on, they always made sure everything was working properly before putting it in me.

I wasn't going to be doing much of anything with all those hoses running this way and that. I had to go through the dressing changes. Yes, they *are* as bad as people say. It stung. *God,* it stung! Then they would start wrapping me up again.

The truth is, I would be at the university hospital for a while. I would have to go through surgery after surgery, and I had months—no, *years*—of rehab ahead of me. The pain was unbearable, and the embarrassment was ongoing, every minute of every day. Think about a team of people examining your most private parts every day and talking about the reconstructive surgery they are hoping to do on them, and you get the idea. Dignity? What is dignity? I hadn't seen what my face looked like yet, but I could see my arms, hands, legs, chest, and privates when my dressings were changed. I knew my face must look pretty bad too.

I think it was the third time they had sewn my eyes shut. I had to have a talk with God. I was pretty good at talking, but not to him. But I spoke to God in my mind the way I would speak to a person.

"God, I can't go on like this. I can't do this."

"You don't have to, Jack."

"What do you mean, God? Can't you just take me home now? You don't know what it's like or how bad I'm hurting. Let me die!"

"No, Jack, you're not going to die. But if you let me, I can carry you."

Later, someone showed me a Bible verse from Isaiah 46:4 that helped me understand: "I have made you and I will carry you. I will sustain you and I will rescue you."

It helped, and I needed help. Every day I was having surgeries of one kind or another, and each time I had to have blood. I had over eighty pints! Sometimes they took me into surgery to debride (remove) dead skin, sometimes to rebuild damaged parts, sometimes cosmetic, and at other times for procedures to help me survive long-term.

Little did I know then, but God had a huge miracle in the works. Most severe burn survivors stay in the burn unit for at least a year. I walked out in only four months and seventeen days. I then went to a Methodist rehab facility in Jackson, Mississippi. I remember the nurse at the rehab facility coming in. I was standing, looking out the window. She asked, "Who is my patient?" She assumed I was bed-bound, as most of her patients were at that point in their journey. I have had some of the best doctors, nurses, and rehabilitation doctors. I am one of the luckiest men in the world. Thank you.

Though I didn't know it at first, A'Leta was journaling the hours and days, keeping a record to share with me later. As we write this book together and I read her entries, it will be the first time I've seen them. At this point, we'll share her first entries with you too.

A'LETA'S FIRST JOURNALS

Sunday, March 5, 2006[12]

You have been in surgery since 1:30 p.m. This is the first of many surgeries, and we are just sitting in the waiting room and praying for you. Brother Danny and Buck Kennedy are here, along with Brian Rayburn and, of course, all of your family. Billy Lee and I saw you right before surgery, and you were doing fine.

The nurse just came in and said you are doing great. They are working on your chest and arms. They are pretty severely burned, but she said you are stable. I am proud of you and how strong you are being.

Baby, I've decided to keep a journal of what you're going through so that someday you and I can read it together. I want to start at the beginning, so I am going back right now to the very first moment that I found out about what happened to you …

Saturday March 4, 12:02 AM

The phone rang, and the caller ID said "Helmerich and Payne" [H&P], so I assumed you were calling me from the rig. I answered the phone and the person on the other end said, "This is Bob Quick. I am sitting in your driveway right now. Open the door." I knew something bad had happened, so I hung up and called Daddy and told him to get over here right now. I freaked out and got up and was shaking all over my whole body. I finally got it together enough to open the door before I lost it. I packed some stuff, and Mr. Bob and Mrs. Peggy put me in the truck and left. On the way, an emergency nurse from Texas called to let me know you were there. She said you were burned on most of your body but that you were responding. She also said they were transporting you to Shreveport. I told her to tell you that I loved you.

When I am in the hospital room with you, I talk to you constantly. But I know that you will not remember any of it. So I am keeping up with all of this for you in a journal so that one day we can sit back and laugh about all of this together while you are holding me and touching me. I miss your voice most of all. Shelley saved my voice mail messages from you so that I can listen to you whenever I want.

Monday, March 6, 2006, 12:16 AM[13]

Baby, I just called Nurse Shannon, and he said you are doing fine. You are going to have surgery tomorrow about 11:00 a.m., and this is the first one of many. They will remove the burned skin on the front part of your body, and you will be in there for about four to five hours. You are doing great and responding well to the pain, and also when I am talking to you. You want me to rub your feet because right now that is the only part of your body that is not bandaged or burned. You are fighting very hard to hold on, and God is giving you that strength. He is giving me the strength to hold up from one minute to the next. You would be so proud of me and how well I am doing through all of this. I love you, and God is giving me strength to live and breathe right now. I really don't want to.

Carney is doing great, and the Lord has got his hands on her. We have not told her what happened yet. We are waiting to do so until we see how you do with surgery. I am going to make notes for you, starting with the very first minute I found out how badly you were hurt, so that when you are ready, I can give them to you and you will know everything in detail.

The boys from the rig came to the hospital today. They are not doing well. I told them that I am very sorry they had to experience what they did, and that I am praying for them daily. Even though I cannot express it in words, I think I know how they feel. They are having some of the same feelings I do, and I do not want them or anyone else feeling like that. You are my hero, and you are fighting so you can come home to your baby girls, and I long for that day. I long for your touch, and we are only in the second day of this. I can only imagine how much I am going to want you to hold me by the time you are able to do that. I love you, and I am going to cry myself to sleep and pray, pray, pray!

Love,
Your Baby Girl

P.S. Carney sent you a note today. I am going to hang it in your room, along with a picture of you and her together. She worships the ground you walk on—and I do, too.

Monday, March 6, 2006, 6:18 PM

The doctor just came in and said your surgery went great. He removed the burned skin from your chest, abdomen, and arms. They will do your backside and legs tomorrow or Wednesday. Yesterday, he told me he was one-hundred percent sure that you would not have any fingers, and that he would have to amputate. I told him that if God wanted you to have them then you would, and that I had faith you would have them. He looked at your fingers and hands today and said they looked much better than yesterday, and that he would *not* have to amputate. Baby, when he told me that I started clapping and praising God. I am so excited. I cannot put the happiness I feel right now in words. I am going to continue to have faith and pray for your full recovery, which I know will happen. The doctor said that you may have some of the tips of your fingers missing, but that he would let them fall off before amputating them because he does not want to interrupt anything that God may have planned. I told him that you would not lose any part of your fingers because I know that God has a plan. And if His plan is to take you home with him to heaven, then I don't believe you would have come this far. I love you, and I am so happy right now I could run five miles because I know that my baby has fingers. I love the fact that God is so making these doctors eat their words.

Kenny Allen said that the boys on the rig are all changed men because of this, so there has been some good to come from it already. Billy Humble saved your life. It took a total of five seconds to shut the rig down, and that was record time. No other driller besides Billy would have been able to make that happen in that short of a period.

Tuesday, March 7, 2006, 4:49 PM

Your second surgery to remove the skin from your legs went well. And your hands are still getting better. I asked the doctor about your ears. They are definitely burned, but he said we are not going to have that discussion because I would just tell him the same thing about the ears that I did with the fingers. Which is true. So I am sure your ears will be fine too.

I "fired" Josh [Jack's good friend][14] today. He almost made me miss my visit with you because he was most worried about himself. I informed him that if I missed my visit, then he would be having surgery with you. It is thrilling to see how God is performing miracles on you daily. You are very strong, and you would not believe how strong I have been.

I miss you, and I will report to you later on a new sexual position I have learned about. I love you. I have got to go so that I can come back and see you.

Wednesday, March 8, 2006

You had a third surgery today on your back and butt. The doc said everything is good and you're doing great. He said he is not doing anything to your hands and that your hands and fingers will be fine. You will have skin grafts on the top of your hands, and fingers, but the palms will be fine and heal themselves.

The upper lip and upper portions of your face are going to be fine and they will heal on their own. The lower lips and the neck will be grafted using the skin from your scalp. They will not do any grafting on your face and neck until Monday. Your ears are burned, and the doc said they will just fall off eventually, but I know that the Lord is going to heal your ears just like he did your hands and fingers. Josh has certainly been a best friend to you. He has not left your side and he is trying very hard to be my personal assistant, even though I have "fired" him many times. He actually has to put color on my hair tonight because it has turned white from all this trauma. I will see you in the morning. Good night and I miss you!

LEARNING TO FORGIVE

A'Leta

Jesus spoke a lot about forgiveness. He must have known how easy it is to hold grudges and how hard it is let go of them.

I can honestly say that Jack didn't seem to be spending his time dwelling on how angry he was at the people who had taken his future away from him. I tried not to stay angry because I knew it was wrong to do so. One day, a couple of months after Jack came home, I wrote about my difficulties in learning to forgive.

November 3, 2006

Today my daily Bible reading was Ephesians 4:32–5:1. The apostle Paul speaks short and straight:

> Be kind and compassionate to one another, forgiving each other, just as in Christ God forgave you. Be imitators of God, therefore, as dearly loved children. (NIV)

We are supposed to forgive others just like Christ forgave us. I am not usually one to hold grudges or to stay mad at someone for something, but knowing that Jack's injuries could have been prevented makes it hard for me just to move on and not have some resentment towards the people who were responsible. There are times when I would love to cost the person or persons responsible more money than they could ever possibly imagine, but I also know that it would not be forgiving to do that. I also know that I am only human, and sometimes the human aspect of things gets the best of and take over my decision-making process. Because of this particular instance and the fact that the company had been making bad stripper rubbers for years and knew it, I feel like money and greed were way more important than my husband's life, my life, and my child's life. Our lives are forever changed, and the life that we worked so hard to build has been snatched away by someone else. It seems they were trying to gain monetarily at the expense of my family. With that thought, it will take a lot of prayer and help from God to move past this.

Looking back, I ask myself, *Have I moved past the bitterness and resentment?* I hope so. Holding onto it hurts the person holding it more than the person it's directed to. I remind myself that God is in control. He didn't cause what happened on March 3rd. People caused it; companies caused it. But God was there with Jack. And he's still there. He's still here.

CHAPTER 14

JUST ANOTHER DAY IN THE BURN UNIT

Jack

Surgery, then so-called recuperation, then surgery again. In the four months and seventeen days I was in the LSU hospital, I underwent around one hundred surgeries. That's not quite one a day, but pretty close.

Dr. Sittig probably saved my life, but I hated him. I was delirious, sometimes so out of it that I was hallucinating. It seemed to me that he was loving and kissing all over A'Leta. It also seemed like he was downright mean—hard core—to the staff. I would get so mad I could have bitten nails. Yet, I couldn't talk. I couldn't do anything. I think now that he did it to make me fight harder.

I think back to the second time the doctors sewed my eyes shut. I could hear everything, but I couldn't see. It was horrifying. Eventually, I worked my eyelids so I could barely see, and that helped me get through that period.

The crazy talk continued once I could actually talk. The staff had a good sense of humor about it. Carney used to sleep with us in our bed before all this happened, and I was sure I was lying on top of her. "Get her out from under me!" I demanded. "Get her out! I'm crushing her!"

One day, coming out of surgery, the nurse we called Mrs. Debbie was pushing me back into my room. "Miss Debbie," I asked, "when can I have sex?"

"Baby, it's gonna be a long time."

"Well, no it ain't," I said. "I'm ready, and you're it!"

Mrs. Debbie was my favorite day nurse. She had to be at least sixty years old! She was embarrassed, but she laughed. Once I realized what I'd said, I was embarrassed too.

I have to pat those nurses on the back again. I had Mr. Shannon at night sometimes, and Miss Jean was with me awhile as well. She was hard on me. She didn't put up with a lot of the crying or whining. She would wrap my feet up. At times, I'd be freezing to death, but she wrapped my feet so well that I could relax and fall asleep.

After a few weeks, I was moved to the convalescent end of the burn unit. A'Leta pushed me to go there. There it meant a quicker release to the rehabilitation center closer to home, but to me it meant I would have to work harder to do the most basic things. It was hard. The nurses would come and get me and prop me up in a wheelchair. It hurt bad just to sit up. All the blood in my body felt as if it were running down to my legs and feet. The pain was agonizing.

Then there were the baths in the hydro/bath room. The torturers—I mean nurses—pulled me out of bed and put me on a stretcher with a rubber mat under it. Then they sprayed water to help loosen the bandages. They used razor blades to cut off all the gauze, peeling it off of me. Then the *real* fun began—I got bathed. They used sponges that felt like wire brushes with soap. If you have ever had a bad cut or a raw place and then sit in a hot tub, you know how it stings all over.

That was painful enough, but the pain was compounded when I had to see my skin. After the hosing down—I mean "bath"—the nurses applied gauze soaked in vinegar or salve to my skin. Then (finally!) dry bandages over that. Then an ACE bandage over that. I'm sure the rest of the wing heard my awful, agonizing, bloodcurdling screams during this time.

Before I forget, I need to describe how I ate. I was right-handed, but that hand was so badly burned that I had to use my left hand. Holding the spoon and moving it to my mouth was so painful that after two or three bites I didn't want any more. It hurt to chew, even though, thankfully, the inside of my mouth was okay. But my mouth was so constricted that I could barely put a peanut M&M into it.

Going to the bathroom was an intense process. The rectal tube that had been inserted while I was still in the ICU was now gone. When I had to go, they would come into the room with a bed pan. One night when my friend Steven was staying with me, I felt the urge to go. The nurse arrived and tried to slide that pan under me, but it was like sliding a wet piece of toilet paper across the carpet. It just rolled up the skin. I started screaming; I couldn't help it. Steven ran out of the room and didn't come back that night. He told me later he could hear me screaming all the way out to the parking lot. Eventually, I got where I insisted they make a diaper-type thing. It was basically three or four absorbent pads so that when I poo'ed, they could just raise my legs, clean me up, and remove one of the absorbent pads. It sounds simple, but it wasn't.

I couldn't pee on my own. If I had to go, someone had to bring in a container and put my privates in it. The first time I was able to go to the bathroom was at LSU. A'Leta was in the room to help me. I peed all over the walls and all over her. We tried to laugh.

And still … A'Leta didn't turn and run out the door, even though she could have. Instead, she wrote down her feelings in the journals she was keeping. She was also keeping a record of my ongoing surgeries. Her perspective on what was happening to me is sometimes different from what I thought was going on. She'll share some more of her notes from those days.

SURGERY AFTER SURGERY: A'LETA'S JOURNALS

Saturday, March 11, 2006, 8:30 PM

A fourth surgery was done yesterday to remove the burned skin from your face and neck. You did fine, and last night you opened your right eye for just a couple of seconds before going back to sleep. Today you slept all day, and I believe that God is constantly healing your body as you sleep. I spent some time with Carney today. We both miss you more than anything right now. Carney draws you pictures, and I will hang them up in your room so you can see them when you decide to open your eyes for me. I am longing for the day that you touch me with the fingers the doctor said you were not going to have. God is seeing these things a little differently.

I broke down when I heard one of our many songs the other day. I tried to listen to "Come a Little Closer," and I couldn't bear to hear it. I will wait and listen to it when you are better and when we can listen to it together—and when you can really come a little closer to me. Once you get to that point, I will never let you go, and I mean it. You will be so sick of me you will not know what to do.

Monday, March 13, 2006, 6:30 PM

First off, let me start with yesterday, March 12, 2006. You stuck your tongue out at me, and then I told you if you stuck it out again I would kiss you. And, of course, without hesitating, you did just that. But I cannot kiss you right now because I could possibly give you an infection, and we do not want anything to slow us down. Other than that, you slept all day yesterday. Shelley, Stephen, Brooke, Regina, Shaun, Josh, and all the family were here yesterday. I had a good day emotionally because they were here to support me.

Today you stuck your tongue out at me four times, and I love it. I told you that is the highlight of my day, and it really is.

The doctor came in and said you are doing great. The surgery you were supposed to have today turned into just a dressing change and cleaning up your face. You will have skin grafts on Wednesday. The doc said he should have enough skin from the lab on April 3 to start the plantings[15] on your chest and abdomen. He said there will be three surgeries to do all that is needed, and he hopes that by April 10 he will be done. You will have to stay in the burn unit for three weeks after that. Then you will be able to go to the convalescent end of the burn unit.

I love you and I want to see your tongue again.

Wednesday, March 15, 5:24 PM

Today you had skin grafts on your lower face and neck. I keep telling you that you got a face lift because it will be wrinkle-free and soft as a baby's butt. You communicated with me this morning before surgery, but since surgery the only thing you have said is, "I love you."

I know God is going to restore you physically and cosmetically. I believe that you are going to look perfect. I keep telling God that I won't accept anything less. Your doctor is going to do another surgery on Friday. You have some pieces on both ears that have broken off, but I still know that God will heal and restore those back to the way they were. Or even better. Your doctor and I often get into arguments over your ears, including today. I keep telling him they are going to be beautiful. He just laughs and says, "No, they're not going to grow

BEFORE PHOTOS

Carney's Fifth Birthday

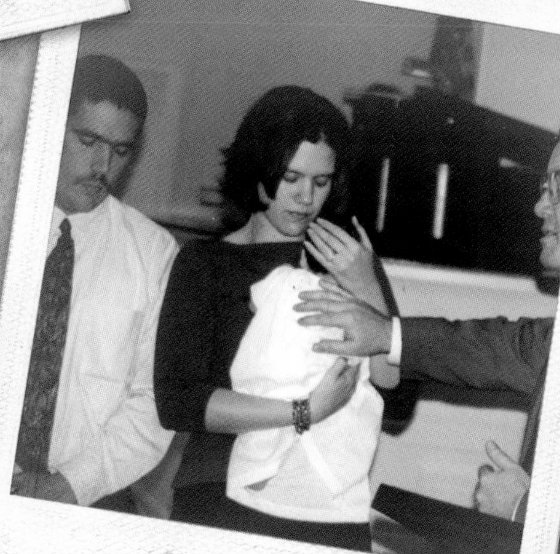

Carney's Dedication Ceremony

Family Trip to Mississippi Gulf Coast

Jack and A'Leta's Dating Years

Jack and A'Leta's Wedding

Family Photo, 2001

Jack and A'Leta's Wedding Kiss

Daddy's Little Girl

Daddy and Daughter Playtime

Christmas 2004

Jack on H&P Rig 72

AFTER PHOTOS

First Time Carney Sat in Daddy's Lap

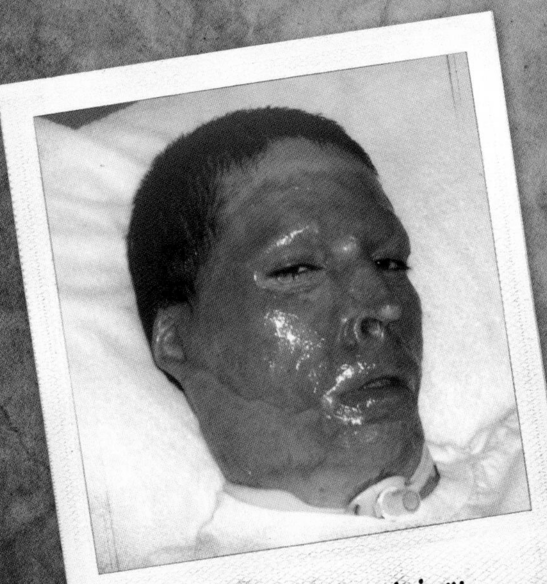

Ten Months After Injury

Jack Hunting

A'Leta and Carney

A'Leta and Carney on Grandfather Mountain, NC

Family Trip to National Aquarium

A'Leta

Easter 2007

Jack, A'leta, and Deirks

Carney and Sidney the Goat

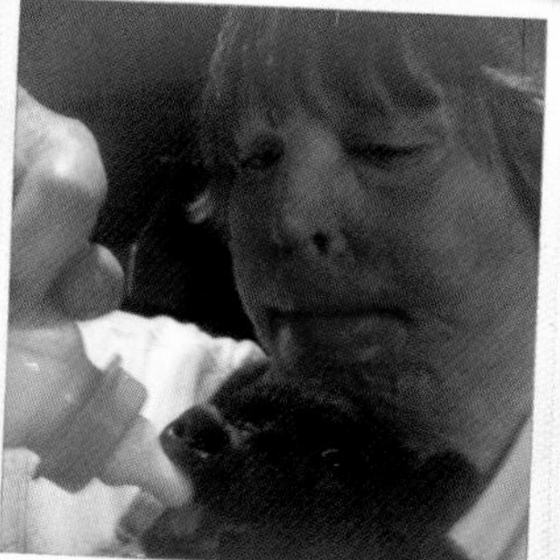

Jack and Gertie the Piglet

Jack, Carney, and A'leta

back." I keep saying, "God can make anything possible, and he is going to do that."

I think your doctor is the greatest ever. He is encouraging, but he does not sugarcoat anything. He tells me like it is and prepares me. After surgery today, he said when I go in to see you that I will scream because of how your grafts look. But that didn't happen. I went in and could not believe how beautiful you looked.

God is really taking care of my attitude and emotions to get me through this minor detour in our life. I know that when this is over you are going to be a vessel for God, and the mighty things that he has in store for you are going to be great. I told Tamyra that when you are ready to go home I will break it to you that we are moving to Honduras to be full-time missionaries! I have told you all along that God has called me to some sort of mission work, and when this is all over we are both going to have many opportunities to serve him in some way. I have already heard from people who want you to come and speak when you are able to do that. God is really working, and I pray that you are not angry with him for what has happened to you. I told God the other night that I could not imagine being in any other place than right where we are. I feel so filled with the Spirit that words cannot express the feelings I have. Only God could make me feel like that in a time like this.

I cannot wait for you to touch me. I know that the day you can finally touch me with your fingertips I will melt in my shoes. I promise you that. I am excited because I know we are going to have an even stronger marriage after this, and a bond that is like no other. It is very special and I feel it, even though I cannot hear your voice or feel your touch. It is still there and I do not believe it will ever go away. Have I told you that I love you?

Friday, March 17, 2006

Let me start with yesterday. [It's been thirteen days since you arrived.] You got off the ventilator, and you are breathing on your own. You also drank a protein shake, but you told me you hated it. The nurse had to come get me out of the waiting room because you would not be still and you told her you wanted your wife. That made me feel good because yesterday morning you did not know who I was, nor did you even know you had a wife. Yet, for the first time you asked me about Carney. You asked, "Where is my baby?"

They are backing you off some of your meds so you are starting to wake up to the real world. I brought you a CD player and a CD. I played "Come a Little Closer" and you started crying. I felt bad because I did not do it to make you cry. I did it to remind you of our favorite song. I understand that the meds make you do and say crazy things. I try my best not to let things bother me. A lot of things you are doing and saying are typical Jack, but I've got to tell you that some things are nuts—but there again, some of the drugs are responsible.

Today you had another very successful surgery. Afterwards, you drank some of a McDonald's shake, and when Shelley came in with me today, you were sticking your tongue out and trying to kiss me. Shelley said, "Hey! I am in the room!"

I am so proud of you and how you are doing. I just wish I knew if you know at this point all that God is doing for us. I have been strong, but only with God's help. I can't cry or have a mental breakdown because I am so happy that God has chosen you to perform maybe one of the greatest miracles that this modern world has ever seen.

It is hard sometimes for me to try being perfect for everyone, but you know how things are with your family sometimes. I am just really tired and I need some privacy. I am tired of being the one everybody walks on. Sometimes I have to say, "Enough is enough."

I know that this really is all about you, not me, and I am faithfully devoting myself to you and your needs and nothing else. I am not letting the Devil in. There is no room for him because God is working miracles every minute on you, and I could not imagine being in any other place. I feel bad about what you have had to go through, and what you are going to go through in the future, but God is giving me a peace and comfort that I cannot explain. It is something I have never felt before. I thank God for choosing me and placing me in this spot—because I think it is an honor. Not every man or woman is chosen for a role like this. He knows that we will allow him to work and will use it for his glory.

Saturday, March 18, 2006

You were very active today. You were awake most of the day and even tried getting out of the bed. Between my visits, you kept asking the nurses for me, and every time I came in you told me I had to take you home and that you had to get up. When I called the night nurse, Shannon, to check on you, he said you had been trying to get up and were kickin' your legs off the side of the bed. I am proud of you and the way you are fighting back. God is healing you by the minute.

Sunday, March 19, 2006

Today you slept all day and did not "talk" to me at all. I think you wore yourself out from moving around so much yesterday. You did pucker up for a kiss. Angela, Austin, Carney, and I went to Broadmoor Baptist Church this morning, They had a prayer for you in the service and then they introduced me to the congregation. Then a lady escorted Angela and me to a Sunday school class with about thirty ladies, all about the age of Mammaw.[16] It was too funny! They had a buffet breakfast and they wanted to make sure that I ate. I told Angela that next Sunday I would go to another, maybe younger, class. About that time, one of the ladies introduced me to the class and announced to the others that I would be with them while I was here in Shreveport. Angela said, "Check the new Sunday school class off your list because these ladies will trample you if they find out you're trying other Sunday school classes!" They were nice—they just want to take care of me. The preacher's wife at Broadmoor has been calling to check on me since the second day you were here. She told me that this summer she would watch Carney for me if I wanted to have Carney here in Shreveport with me. I am probably going to do that if things work out.

I love you more than you can imagine. You keep telling me that you are sorry for all this, but I know you do not realize how honored and extremely thankful I am that God has chosen our family to perform such an awesome miracle. I know that millions of people will be affected by what he does in your life. Who knows? We might even be able to write a book after all this.

Monday, March 20, 2006

Today you had skin grafts on your right hand. They took the skin from one of your ankles and used it on your wrist, hands, thumb, and pinky finger. The doctor said that the middle fingers would heal on their own. Everything went very well, and you did great. You slept most of the rest of the day. I love you with all my heart and I am amazed at how God is working with you.

Tuesday, March 21, 2006

Today you were not active and just about slept all day. But according to Shannon you were very active during the night. You are not sleeping that much at night, but that is not new. At one point you did wake up and asked me, "Where is Carney? Is she okay?" You also asked me today why I was "running from you." Drugs make you say and do crazy things.

When I go into your room I feel the presence of God immediately. I hope you feel the same Presence and that you are at peace with everything that has happened. I am extremely tired and that is why some of these journal entries are not very lengthy. They will get better once I catch up on some sleep.

Wednesday, March 22, 2006

Dr. Sittig just came in and talked to me about the surgery you had today. He did the grafts on your bottom and on the top of your left hand. He is still concerned about the pinky and middle finger to the first joint. He said he will not amputate those until the very end. I told him that God will heal them and make them perfect. I am asking God to make you perfect again. You are not sleeping that well, but they will not give you anything for it at this point. The doc doesn't seem to be concerned about that. I did tell him today that you had a torn rotator cuff from an earlier injury so that physical therapy would probably help.

You are my precious Baby.

Thursday, March 23, 2006

This was another good day for you. The main thing is that you did not have any surgeries. They started you on some anti-anxiety medications called Zyprexa[17] and Ativan to try to help you sleep and to stop the hallucinations, but I don't think either one of them is working very well. You were saying some crazy stuff after they gave them to you, and you told me that you have never felt like that before. You told me at the 7:15 p.m. visit to come get in the bed with you. You said, "I know you can't kiss me, but at least you can touch me."

You asked me, "Where is Lemuel? I need to talk to him," so I called him and he is coming tomorrow night to see you. I am sorry you have to endure all of this physical and emotional excruciating pain. Sometimes when I am in the room with you, I want to cry because of the things you say under the influence of the medication, and also because of some of the expressions on your face. When that happens, you are clearly not my man. I know that God is going to take care of that, just like he is taking care of the physical part for you.

I think when you go to the long-term care facility when you get out of here that it is going to be just you, me, and Carney. I will still have a scheduled visiting time, and I will not be able to spend the night there because you will be in therapy all the time. Besides, Carney will be getting out of school shortly, and I'll need to be there with her.

Don't mind me. Right now, I am just venting. I am sick and tired, and I need you. I want you to get well so we can go home. I think you are the strongest man that I know or ever will know. You are my world, and I know that our relationship will be forever changed because of this life-changing, traumatic event that is happening. I will have a love and respect for you that I have never known before, and I think you will have that same love and respect for me that you have never known before.

Friday, March 24, 2006

Today Dr. Sittig reharvested part of your scalp and put it on the back of your neck. You did great during that surgery. The Zyprexa you started on yesterday made you mean, and you cursed the nurse. You did not curse me, but you were cursing almost everyone else. You told the nurse,[18] "Get this &@^! tube out of my throat, and get out of my &@^! room!" You told me you felt terrible. They stopped the Zyprexa and then gave you Haldol,[19] which is supposed to help you tell the difference between real things and things that are imaginary. But that medicine made you start crying.

I got upset and told Dr. Sittig that I wanted you off antipsychotic drugs, and he said that was fine. He said we would just give you pain meds for now. They started you on them because you were having hallucinations and you had not slept in three days. You were being very mean. I told you, "Lay in that same spot, do not move, and do not open your mouth until I get back." You did what I told you, but then everyone started fussing at me for saying something like that to you. But I knew you would listen to what I said if I said it with some authority, and I did *not* want you cursing your nurse or anyone else.

Today has been stressful. I had to deal with United Blood Services about getting your thirteen pints of blood over here that were given in direct donation for you. They wanted $3200 from Workers' Comp, and they had not discussed this with Workers' Comp until now.

Dr. Sittig said he was worried about me. He said, "This is not one of those major downfalls that I keep warning you about. This is just one of those little minor bumps in the road. It worries me that you're not smiling and laughing."

I told him I was fine and that I had gotten everything straightened out. I had just had it today. As for the major downfalls he has warned me about, I told him there were not going to be any. He said, "If there is not, Jack will be the first burn patient that has ever come through my unit that has not had one."

I said, "Well, Jack will be the first. And God has a plan here and he is showing us daily that Jack is going to do things that no other burn patient with his extent of burns and damage has ever done."

He said, "I know that, and I hope that is the case."

God is working a huge, miraculous miracle right before our eyes. The nurses tell me everyday that they have never seen a burn patient burned as bad as you survive, much less doing as well as you are. What can I say? You know I love you and God must love you too!

Saturday, March 25, 2006

Today was quiet and so were you. You were calm because all the crazy drugs are out of your system. A man by the name of Dick Green came to see you today. He works for BP, and he just found out about what happened to you. He came in with me and talked to you. You said you remembered him, and you told me to tell him to leave some money before he left! I keep telling you that H&P and their employees are doing everything they can to take care of us. The community is also donating. Dick brought his wife with him. They live here in Shreveport and they said if I need anything at all that they would be here and get me whatever I needed. I miss you and I can't wait to see you tomorrow.

Sunday, March 26, 2006

You are doing well today. You are starting to put some of the puzzle pieces together about where you are, how long you will be here, and what day and time of day it is. You are being very cocky and cursing pretty uncontrollably, and I keep telling you to please stop that trashy talk. Of course, I understand it is the medicine talking. You get frustrated, and you act like you want to hit me. That bothers me because it's not the normal you.

Actually, we did have a normal adult conversation today. I asked you if you knew how badly you were burned, and you said, "Yeah, ninety-five percent of my body is burned."

I asked, "Do you know God was with you?" I told you that God literally carried you through the explosion while it was happening and the minutes shortly thereafter.

You said, "Yeah, I know he was there, and he was there when he blew my @*$ up."

It took all I had not to laugh and/or cry at that moment, but I did not. I said, "You know that God has a plan."

You said, "Yeah, he planned it before I was ever born."

> Your eyes saw me when I was formless; all my days were written in Your book and planned before a single one of them began.
>
> —Psalm 139:16 HCSB

"Do you know why he chose you?"

"Yeah, I am the only one who can handle it."

"That's right, and God knew I was the only wife who could handle it with you. Do you resent God, Jack?"

"No, I know it was part of his plan."

I talked to you about H&P. You said you knew that it was not their fault and that you did not blame them. Then I asked, "Do you know what caused the rig to blow up, Jack?"

You said, "Yeah, it was the stripper rubber, and I know whose fault it was."[20]

I will stop for today. I love you. I pray and have faith you are not going to blame God, and I pray you are going to serve God and fulfill the plan that he has for you and our family.

Monday, March 27, 2006

According to Dr. Sittig, you are doing great—that is, considering your injuries. They started giving you solid foods today and you tolerated them well. You stayed up almost all day, and I got to spend a pretty good bit of time with you. They are going to start you on sleeping pills tonight and see if that will help you get some needed sleep. You have been asking for your cell phone for two days now so that you can call your daddy. Your daddy has been to see you, and he calls every morning and talks to the nurses. The nurses keep telling you when he calls, but you keep forgetting. He has seen you and talked to you, but you do not remember. Today you are asking for Bob Quick because you want to see him. He is coming in a couple of days. I just got off the phone with Bob, and he is supposed to go work on a rig tomorrow. But since I told him that you were asking for him all day today, he said he is probably coming tomorrow. I am so proud that you are doing great.

Tuesday, March 28, 2006

You slept all night last night for the first time in a couple of weeks. I think you were much more relaxed today than you have been. Josh, Bulldog, and Kenny came to see you today. The nurse told us you tried getting out of the bed this morning, and when she came in your room you were sitting on the floor. She said she didn't think you fell. She thinks you realized you couldn't walk yet, and so you just sat down! The doctors and nurses are all amazed at how fast you are progressing. I think you have an audience at times throughout the day because the hospital staff comes in just to look and marvel. You are a sight.

You had your first shower in the car wash [a room in the burn unit called "Hydro," where the showering and dressing changes are done daily on burn patients]today. And you had several bowel movements, so Dr. Sittig sent a culture off to see if you have some sort of infection. Bulldog was back there with me when I was talking to him. I said, "Dr. Sittig, this is Jack's normal schedule. He goes four or five times a day."

He said, "You have got to be kidding me."

Bulldog backed me up and said you go at least four times a day when you are working on the rig.

The doctor thought that was pretty funny. He said, "We have a hose we can stick up there to take care of that." I told him he might want to go ahead with that because you are very regular. I told them all that you have never been stopped up before, so I did not see why you would start now. I actually apologized to the nurse because she had to clean you up three times that I know of today. She said it does not bother her. She is just glad you can actually go! She said it is usually very hard to get patients to start bowel movements because of the medications, and also because it has been so long since they have had solid foods. She thinks it's great that we do not have to make you go.

You did not want me to leave you tonight. I am sorry that I can't spend the night with you, but they will not let me. I will see you in the morning, and I'll even bring the McDonald's French fries you've been asking for.

Wednesday, March 29, 2006

You had a temp today and had to be put back on oxygen. You were not taking deep enough breaths to keep your lungs clear. Your chest X-ray was normal, but you are coughing up a lot of stuff. They are checking cultures for infections because of the fever. This has not been a good day for you. You feel lousy and you cried a lot today because you are more alert and reality is hitting you.

Bob came today, and you got very upset with him. You told him you wanted to make sure you still have a job when you get out and that your girls are being taking care of. He told you that it is his responsibility now to make sure that Carney and I are okay and for you not to worry about it. After Bob, Shakey came to see you too. The doctor said that all of the emotions are good (like your getting upset with Bob) because it means that you are more coherent. In fact, today you wanted to know about when your skin will be here, when they will start surgery, and how long it will be before we know if the skin is going to take or not. Anyway, again you did not want me to leave you at the end of the day. That is how I know that you are becoming more aware.

Thursday, March 30, 2006

Baby, you are doing great today. You did not sleep at all last night so you slept this morning. You spelled out that you want to know details about your surgery and your recovery. I told you today that you might lose your pinky on the left hand. That is what I was told, but I really think God is going to heal that for you. You looked at me funny when I told you about the finger, but I don't want to lie to you and I am not going to. If you ask me something, I will tell you the truth. The third day you were here, Dr. Sittig told me he was absolutely certain you would lose all your fingers, and maybe parts of your hands. But God saw things a little differently, and the next day Dr. Sittig said your fingers looked one-hundred percent better than the day before. You will have all of your fingers!

God is healing you, though I know you do not realize that yet. The doctor said that you would not make it through the day on March 4, but you did. I argued with him that morning and I told him God was going to heal you. I have not stopped since. I am praying for you and fighting for you every step of the way. I really miss you tonight. I am lonely and I really need you to hold and touch me. Even though I miss you, and at times it feels unbearable, I stay strong and never cry about it. I know that one day I am going to have to take time and grieve and let it all out, but at this point I do not have the time to do that. I am so thankful that you are alive and doing so well that I feel like grieving would be selfish of me. God is comforting me and making me stronger than I thought I could ever be. I am so proud of you for taking things in stride and doing great in your recovery. I love you very much, baby!

Friday, March 31, 2006

You had a crying spell this morning, but after that you had a good day. I called Daddy and held the cell phone up to your ear so he could talk to you. You told him you felt better. You have not slept in two days, so you do get upset and frustrated often. I love you and miss you so much. I want you to hold me and kiss me all over.

You wanted to know about your surgery again today. You are scared and understandably you want to know all of the details. I keep telling you that we are over the scary part, and that you slept through all of it. The worst part was the first seventy-two hours, when the doctors were not sure if you would live. Yet, I knew you were going to live because I prayed and asked God to intervene, and I had faith he was going to do what I asked. And he did. He is working miracles on you constantly, and I am amazed at how you are doing. I love you and I will see you tomorrow.

Sunday, April 1, 2006

When I came in today you were very aware and talking to me with the alphabet board without any problems. Though you were having gas pains and hurting all over, you really were doing well. You are upset and scared about the surgery. The nurses and I keep telling you that it is not that bad, and once you have some of your own skin in place the risk of infection will lessen. Early on, the doctors warned me about your picking up major infections, but you have not had any. We are so blessed. You did not want to see anyone tonight at the 7:15 p.m. visit. You told me to go tell everybody in the waiting room to go home and for me to come back and stay with you. When it came time for me to leave, neither of us wanted that. I can hardly wait to see you tomorrow.

Jack comments on those days ...

Some of my memories of these early days might best be told by A'Leta, but I do remember the frantic feeling I had about getting back to work. I was afraid I'd lose my job. My supervisor, Bob Quick, came to visit me. He assured me that my job would be taken care of, that it wasn't an issue. Still, I kept thinking, *I have to hurry up and get back to the rig. I have to hurry ...*

Sunday, April 2, 2006

You had your eleventh surgery today, and it was the first one to start the plantings of the cultured skin. They removed the pig skin from your chest, abdomen, and both arms, and tomorrow they will cover those areas with the cultured skin. The surgery today went very well and you did great. When you started coming out from under the anesthesia you got confused, and the nurse [Terri] had to put you in restraints because you were trying to get up. She came and got me out of the waiting room twice because she could not do anything with you. She said that when I come in you get a lot calmer.

I left the hospital and went back to the hotel while your mom stayed with you until I got back. When I got back, she told me she was glad I was there because she also couldn't do anything with you! She said that all you wanted was your wife and you were shouting out for me. I came in with you and you calmed down and went to sleep. You told me that you did not want to see anybody at the next visiting hour because you wanted to go to bed. You told me later today that you were yelling [just making noise because Jack was still unable to talk at this point because of trache] because you figured out the nurses would come get me out of the waiting room to come back there and deal with you.

You got upset tonight during my last visit, and you were crying because you had gas again. You were really hurting. I hate to come in your room and you start crying, but there is nothing I can do about that. You hurt and I am helpless. The hardest thing for me is not the fact that this horrible thing happened to you or seeing how you look in your burned condition. The hardest thing for me is the fear I see in your eyes and the knowledge that I can say or do nothing to make it better. I always seem to be able to talk you through it, and you do calm down, but I think that as soon as I leave you start again because you do not want to get me upset. The doctor said today that you will probably be in the ICU for about another three to four weeks, and then you will go to a regular room for a few weeks. After that, it looks like you may be going to a long-term care facility.

I love you and miss you, and I will never leave your side.

Monday, April 3, 2006

You had your cultured skin put on your chest, abdomen, both arms, shoulders, and right leg up to the mid-thigh section. You did fine once you got to sleep. Afterward, while you were coming off the anesthetic, the nurses again had to come get me to handle you. You kept telling me to put the truck in park and to untie your arms [they are bandaged]. You are in an airplane position that I know has to be very uncomfortable, but I keep telling you to be thankful that you have limbs. Going through what you went through could have very easily meant you had no limbs. After surgery, you kept telling me to kiss you on the mouth. You told me to take your mask off so you could kiss me. I would love to kiss you and hold you because I miss you and can't wait until we go home together.

You are the man of my dreams, and I am so happy you chose me to be your wife.

Tuesday, April 4, 2006

Today was another good day for you, even though you did not sleep last night. You ate mashed potatoes, chicken, and pears today. I am amazed at your progress. You are the strongest man on the face of the earth.

Bulldog, Billy Humble, and Kenny came to see you today, and Billy and Bulldog came in your room to see you. I told you when I left today that your lips look so good since they have healed, and that it would not be long before I could suck your lips off. You smiled and "said" you couldn't think about it right now, and then you told me to change your TV. [All this time I had been reading Jack's lips to communicate because of his inability to talk. God undoubtedly gave me that gift at the exact time I needed it because I did not previously possess this gift. God is an on-time God!]

You are doing so much better tonight than you did last night. Last night they gave you a beer with your sleeping pill, but it did not work. So tonight I think they are going to give you two beers and a sleeping pill. I told them I did not care how many beers it takes as long as you get some rest. I cannot wait to see you in the morning. I miss you way too much.

Wednesday, April 5, 2006

They changed your trache today and put the metal piece in so you can get some better sound out now. You are doing better than expected, but you still have not slept. I just called and Shannon [a nurse] said you were joking with him. You told him you were ready to "get this $#!^ off of me and go home." I told him to tell you I called to check on you and that I loved you. I told him to tell you that I said you better go to sleep. We prayed together tonight before I left, and you said you were ready to go to sleep.

We toured Life Care today. That is the long-term care facility you wanted to know all about. It is a nice facility and it looks like a small hospital. If you wind up there, Carney will be allowed to come and visit. According to your doctor, you will be going there in about five weeks. You will be there maybe two months before we can go home.

Now, go to sleep.

Thursday, April 6, 2006

Today you are having no trouble talking with sound coming out, and you are aware of everything going on. You met Lisa. She is the counselor who is going to start meeting with you regularly. You ate very well today, and I am just so proud of you. You told me you wished you could hold Carney. Words cannot express how much we love you!

You told me that when you were on fire, you were trying to jump off the board to get away. I asked you why you didn't, and you said God held you up there and wouldn't let you jump. You said you wanted to die, but then you changed your mind and decided you wanted to live. You said God was right there with you the whole time.

Friday, April 7, 2006

Your condition gets better and better each day. The counselor met with you, and you asked her to come back tomorrow. I am going to spend some time with Carney tomorrow, so I will not come up there until the afternoon. I told you that Daddy, Billy Lee [Jack's cousin], and Mug [another relative] were going to take care of you while I was gone, and you said that would be fine. You had a look on your face like you were very concerned. I asked you if you would be okay, and you said you did not know. I know you want me there all the time, and I also know that you understand that I have to spend time with Carney as well. Thank you for being so very strong.

The night nurse told me I had to leave tonight. She is not very nice, but compared to the last one she is like sunshine. Still, she was just not working out, and so I finally complained enough until they moved her. I do not think you remember any of this because you were out of it at the time. I will miss you until tomorrow.

Saturday, April 8, 2006

What I said yesterday about your condition getting better and better each day does not apply today. I was not going to come to the hospital until the afternoon because I had planned to spend some time with Carney. Daddy, Billy Lee, Mug, and your mom were there with you. Your mom told me you were not having a good day, so I came up there and spent four hours in the room with you by myself (standing on the hospital floor that entire time), just talking to you and trying to comfort you and get you to calm down. You do better when I am in there, and you did get calmer when I arrived. But you were confused and fighting everyone, and you did not know anybody or anything. To make a long story short, it was an emotional day, not really with you but mostly with your family. I just want you to know that I love you and I will be here until I can take you home with me. I married you and I made a promise to you, and I intend to follow through with that regardless of who gets their feelings hurt.

I am like a robot right now, and my feelings are numb. Besides doing my duties as a wife and mother and caring for you and sleeping, everything else is a blur. I am not concerned about my feelings and I am not concerned about anybody else's feelings, except for yours and Carney's. Regardless of what anybody thinks is right or wrong, I am the head of our household right now, and it is my responsibility to make the decisions. And that is what I intend to do.

From this day forward, I do not care if it is your family or mine, but I am not going to let people run over me, period. I am tired of people coming in that room and telling me I do not feed you right; I do not pick the skin off your face right; I do not help you drink right; and I don't make the right decisions regarding your health care or your best interest.

You asked your nurse today when you could have sex, and she told you it would be awhile. You told her you were ready right now. It's kind of funny, but you were calling Carney "Carney Junior" all day, and you were talking about our two kids. Daddy and I laughed and laughed, and you were looking at us like we were the crazy ones. You called John Sandifer on your pretend cell phone and told him to come to the LSU burn center right now—and to bring Tim McGraw with him. You were cursing nonstop all day long. They gave you Demerol[21] and Phenergan[22] for the first time, and they did not phase you.

Baby, I love you, and being with you and caring for you is all I want to do. I do not want to think about anything else. All this other crap is just adding unnecessary stress, and I am over it. I don't even care.

Sunday, April 9, 2006

Your surgery today is to remove the rest of the pig skin on your right leg and all of it on your left leg. Tomorrow they will put on the cultured skin in those areas. They put a stitch in your eyelids because you can't completely close them anymore, and this is to keep the corneas from drying out. I know it is miserable for you, and I explained to you that it was going to help your eyes in the long run. They bandaged your entire face for this procedure, and you are confused about what is going on. They did this so your face can dry out and heal faster. You got some good rest most of the day because they are keeping you on mild anesthesia. I love you and I'll see you tomorrow.

Thursday, April 13, 2006

I have skipped a few days in my journal because you have not had a surgery since Monday, and every day since has pretty much been the same.

When they check you every day during dressing changes (they take you into surgery to do these dressing changes), they find that you have more and more new skin cells, and they are amazed at how fast your skin is growing. You are complaining a lot about the pain, however, and I am praying the doctors can come up with a medicine that will work better. You are so strong. God is doing great work with your body. In fact, unless people are here to witness your progress firsthand, they probably think I am nuts when I tell them about it. Because of your injuries, God is showing himself through our family, and I am so thankful this is happening.

You do not want me to leave your room, and every time you wake up you send the nurse out to the waiting room to get me. If I am not there, they call me on the cell phone to let me know you are awake and that you want me to come translate for you. No one can understand what you are saying, and I think that is another miracle from God because he is giving me the gift to be able to understand you. You only want me in there with you, and you really do not want much family or friends right now.

We all love you and miss you so much. I cannot wait to hold you and feel you holding me back.

CHAPTER 16

MELTDOWNS AND ADJUSTMENTS

A'Leta

It is time to confess something that was apparent as I look at my journal entries at the end of April: I was about to lose it. April 24 was a particularly trying day for Jack, and because it was hard for him, it was hard for me. I describe it in my journal:

Wednesday, April 24, 2006

You had plastic surgery today on your eyes for the second time, and they stitched them up again for the third time. That is aggravating for you. They also took the skin from your abdomen to graft most of your left leg and finish the right leg. You are very down and cried a lot today and during the night. You are on the fourth day and third night with no sleep. You are seeing things and you feel like you are spinning. It is due to a combination of things: the infection, the eyes being stitched, and the lack of sleep. You told me yesterday that you did not want to live anymore and to tell Carney that you [A'Leta] love her, but that her daddy is not strong enough to take this life. You want to die because you cannot take the pain any longer.

> It is very difficult for me to stay strong and to listen to this without crying, but inside I am actually dying. I know that God has a plan, and I am trying to stay focused. But sometimes when I have time to sit and think, which is not very often, I wonder why he chose us and if there is ever going to be light at the end. The Christian part of me knows that we will be stronger because of this, but the human in me thinks that I will never make it to see the reward God has for us on this earth.

Even with the support we received from family, friends, pastors, and even people we didn't know who were praying for us, there were days when I could barely handle the stress, and days when I felt I couldn't handle it at all. No one knew how I was feeling. I kept it to myself, but I recorded my thoughts. I wrote about a very dark day on May 23, 2006:

> Last week my whole family had a meltdown. We have all realized that we have got to face the tragedy that has happened and is still happening every day. We have got to come to terms with our life. Jack, Carney, and I have reached a low that we have no idea how to get out of. Jack is extremely depressed and wants to give up. He is tired of being physically and mentally disabled or limited. He is tired of not being accepted by the outside world.
>
> Carney and I both feel that we are not accepted because of Jack and our life. Carney cannot do even a basic task without having a meltdown. She is not coping at all with anything. Dr. Bishop told us we should homeschool this year[23] because she has got to rest and heal. She is not able to be resilient anymore.
>
> I hope that we can all rest and try to heal. We have to, or our family will fall apart. We are at a place that we have never been before in our lives. These feelings cannot be explained or understood. I hope that with prayer and me making myself deal with our life that we can get it together. Carney is not able to get it together on her own, and at this point Jack and I are not mentally able to help her.
>
> Dr. Bishop started her on an antidepressant last week. She doesn't sleep and she is not functioning well. Jack cannot sleep and Dr. Grissom added Xanax to his meds. I go to Dr. Bishop, and who knows? He may add something to mine. I feel like we need to go to a

mental institution but that would be the easy way. We have to learn and make ourselves adjust to this life and to make the best of it that we possibly can. That is way easier said than done. Our only hope right now is allowing God to carry us through this because we are not able to do it right now. I do have the faith that He will and we have to allow Him as a family to do it.

May was a difficult month in yet another way. I was growing more and more worried about Carney. My journals describe the challenges:

May 23, 2006

You have not slept for three nights, and you have been saying some crazy things. Yesterday I asked the resident to check your blood cultures for an infection. He said they would watch you closely, and that there was not a reason to do that. The last infection that you had, you did not spike a fever until five days of no sleep and you were severely psychotic. Dr. Richardson came in this morning and said they did check them yesterday, and they were positive. They are starting you on more antibiotics today and hopefully in a couple of days that will be under control.

You seem to be getting down. You had a nerve conduction study on your right arm, and you do have nerve damage but it did not show where. We will see what the next step is when we talk to Dr. Richardson. I know you are getting frustrated, and I am so sorry that you are having to go through such mental and physical pain. It has got to be the hardest thing that any one human being can go through. You fed yourself yesterday, so you are having some progress. Even though the nerve damage and having to start all over on the skin grafts on the back side of your body seem like setbacks, there is some progress going on.

Monday, May 29, 2006

Your infection is gone and they took some of your stitches out on Saturday. Your eyes look good and you can close them now. The plastic surgeon is going to do surgery on your mouth this week because you cannot close your mouth or open it very much, which makes it hard for you to eat or drink from a straw. You are feeling pretty good. We are still waiting on donor sites to heal so they can finish covering your body with skin for the second time. I love you and I am very proud of you.

Tuesday, May 30, 2006

You slept well last night from 10 p.m. to 9 a.m. this morning, but you do not feel very good. You are being very short with me and crying a lot. The psychiatrist is starting you on a new antidepressant today, and you are taking something for the nightmares and flashbacks. You are upset with me because your mom is going to stay with you tonight (instead of me), but I am not feeling good. I am having some problems with my stomach.

I never dreamed that we would have to go through such a traumatic time at such a young age. I keep preparing myself that this is only the beginning, and we have many more years of this left to go. I am praying that God will continue to give me the strength to be there for you and to care for you. I am praying that he will continue to heal you and that he will give you the strength that you need to get through this.

Thursday, June 1, 2006

You had plastic surgery today on your mouth to release your bottom lip so that you can open and close your mouth better. [This will have to be done numerous times in the coming years.] You had a horrible time after surgery. You cried and screamed for about two hours before they could find some meds to relieve the pain some. You are very tired and depressed. You have post traumatic stress syndrome, so the doctors are working with you on that and playing with some meds to try to stop the nightmares, hallucinations, and the depression.

You sat up today in the cardiac chair for most of the day. Right now we are trying to get you more physical therapy on a regular basis. I feel like the PTs think you have plenty of time to start that and they put you off. I am getting very frustrated and have talked to the therapist, doctors, and nurses to try to get some progress started. You get your occupational therapy pretty much every day, but it is past time for you to start sitting up and getting you to stand so that you can take some steps. Dr. Richardson said we might be able to go home in about four weeks, but if you do not start getting the therapy you need, it will not happen.

By this time, three months after the explosion, I hit a plateau of loneliness and fatigue. I sat down one day and wrote out a list of things I loved about Jack. I ended the list with these words: "It is the smallest things that I miss more than anything in the world. The things that I never thought about and took for granted prior to this horrible tragedy. I cannot even think or type right now because I am crying so hard. I love him. I miss my Jack and everything about him."

Meanwhile, Jack was having his own issues with depression. He would cry for hours and hours, or he'd get short with me, or he'd be extremely demanding. He didn't want me to leave his room at all.

Yet, I finally had to. I explain why in my entry from June 2:

June 2, 2006

You cried a lot last night and most of the day today. I am flying home tomorrow morning for Carney's dance recital for the first time since I got here on March 4. I am looking forward to going home and just sleeping in my own bed. I promised myself when I got here that I would not be back home until the day that you could go home with me, but I have to be there for Carney. I miss her more than anything. I just want to be with her and be there for her every day, and it hurts so bad that I can't. I know that you need me right now more than you need or want anybody else, but she is only six. I am scared that when she gets older she is going to say, "Well, you abandoned me and just packed up and left and didn't come back for four months." Kids remember things differently than what really happened, but at six, that is probably what she feels like. I know that God is going to take care of everything and he is still in control, but knowing that, my heart still hurts. I love you and I hope that I am doing the right thing as a mother, at the same time that I know that I am doing the right thing as your wife.

We were beginning to wear on each other's nerves. I didn't tell Jack the things I was writing, but I think they were bothering him too. He took out his frustrations on the person nearest to him—me. I understood this. I was able to express how I felt in my journals, without unloading on him:

June 13, 2006

> You and I had a heated conversation and we were both upset. I hate that because I do not want you to be worried about anything except getting better to come home. I want so bad to have an adult conversation with my husband, the one that left me on March 3, 2006, at 11 p.m., not by choice but by an explosion that almost took your life. I know that it was in God's plan, but I sometimes just want to be mad at the people who could have prevented this but chose not to. They ripped my heart from me and took Daddy away from our six-year-old daughter. This is truly the hardest thing I have ever experienced, and I pray really hard and try my best to be the wife you need right now. I miss you telling me a million times a day that you love me and how beautiful I am. I know that one day I will have that back because I have the faith in God and you that you will be one-hundred percent one day.
>
> I want our child to have a normal life again, with two parents at home to take care of her and for her to feel safe. I am not even sure that my child feels safe right now. She says that she is, but I am not real sure. I want to go home with you. I want you to talk to me and for me to feel like I am the only person in the world. But for right now I just live with the great memories that we have made together when you were able to think outside of yourself.

One of Jack's biggest worries was about how Carney would feel about him. Would she shy away from him? Would she want to be close to him? On May 30, I wrote,

"Carney is coming around a little bit more. She is wanting to talk to you when she calls, and not me that much. She did talk to you a little more when she came to see you on Saturday. She will not be back for about two weeks. I hope that does not cause her to have to start all over as far as coming to see you."

Carney had become hesitant about seeing her daddy. I don't have to explain why. For a child not yet seven years old, it was too much for her.

On June 9, Jack had another surgery, in which the doctors took skin from his scalp to graft onto his legs. He was becoming a patchwork quilt of grafts by that time. When I read this entry, I am amazed that his scalp was the site of the skin they harvested. He was starting to walk a little. Carney came to visit, and what she did that day cheered him up. It also gave a boost to my faltering faith:

June 9, 2006

You have walked with the help of the PT during the last two days. You fed yourself yesterday and I took you outside yesterday for the first time. Carney came in your room today and visited with you and kissed you on your cheek. You were crying tears of joy because all week you have been worried that Carney is not going to want anything to do with you or want to hug you anymore because of your scars.

That was another miracle God performed this week for you. You feel so much better for that. I am so proud of how much you have accomplished just in the past couple of days. I knew you could do it and that you were going to do it. From day one I have told anybody who would listen that Jack is the strongest man I know, and when it comes to the therapy you are going to do it, he'll do it better and faster than anyone else could possibly do it. I love you and I am very proud of you.

There would be many more days of blues, questions, resentfulness, and depression ahead for Jack and me. In spite of them, I knew this: There was nothing in our lives that would ever be the same as it was before March 3, 2006.

But with the help of God, we could do it and become stronger because of it.

OPERATIONS AND MORE OPERATIONS

A'Leta

Many of my journals have been logs of the procedures Jack went through. I knew that someday he'd want to know what had been done and when. (Even with us writing this book, Jack has yet to read many of my journal entries. He is still not ready, and he may never be.) For me, keeping records also acted later as a testimony of God's presence in almost unbelievable situations.

While he was in the hospital Jack received *eighty-three pints* of blood. He has had one hundred ten surgeries thus far. Some have been debriding procedures or other "routine" (as if anything for a patient burned over ninety-five percent of his body is routine) procedures. The list below does not record all of these procedures, but it describes some of the procedures I noted in my journals:

- March 5: First surgery; work on chest and arms
- March 6: Remove the burned skin on the front part of his body
- March 7: Second surgery to remove skin from legs

- March 8: Third surgery on back and butt
- March 10: A fourth surgery to remove the burned skin from face and neck
- March 15: Skin grafts on lower face and neck
- March 17: Taken off ventilator, breathing on own
- March 20: Skin grafts on right hand
- March 22: Grafts on butt and on the top of left hand
- March 24: Re-harvested part of scalp, put it on back of neck
- April 2: Started plantings of cultured skin—removed the pig skin from chest, abdomen, and both arms
- April 3: Covered those areas with cultured skin—chest, abdomen, both arms, shoulders, and right leg up to the mid-thigh section
- April 5: Changed trache and put a piece in it so he could talk a little
- April 9: Removed the rest of the pig skin from right leg and all of it on left leg
- April 10: Put on the cultured skin in those areas, stitched eyelids closed to keep the corneas from drying out
- April 24: Second plastic surgery on eyes—stitched them shut again
- May 23: Removed stitches
- June 1: Plastic surgery today on mouth to release bottom lip so he can open and close his mouth better
- December 18: Surgery on his lips—slit the sides and cut some of the scar tissue out so that he can open his mouth more
- December 28: Stitches removed
- January 29, 2007 (approximately): Steroid injections in scar tissue in mouth to loosen up scar tissue
- March 11: Neck-release surgery
- March 12: Cut chin to release it
- April 12: Large piece of skin grafted from his stomach to his neck

- November 9: Neck release, cut from one side of his neck to the other in the front and left open for about four inches—faux skin on and in four weeks will graft it—stapled it and stitched a bolster on it all the way around
- December 7: Graft on his neck
- January 25, 2008: Liposuction, fat injections, and trache taken out (finally!)
- October 2009: Three major surgeries in one on face, neck, thumb on right hand (six-week recuperation in San Antonio, Texas)

There were many days while in the burn unit at LSU that Jack was taken to the operating room for dressing changes, all while under anesthesia. It does not get easier the more surgeries he has. In fact, it gets worse. There is always the fear of complications during surgery—the more you have, the higher the risk. Thank God we have been spared thus far from a bad scare from a surgery or anesthesia.

CHAPTER 18

I SAW A MONSTER

Jack

I was a smoker before the oil-rig incident. As I lay in that bed, swathed in bandages, I dreamed I was smoking cigarettes, and they were burning my face or fingers. But I still wanted a smoke. One time, when my stepbrother, Chad, and my dad, Jacky, came to visit me, I smelled cigarette smoke. Maybe I smelled it on him—or maybe it was another hallucination—but I was "smoking." I sort of woke up and said, "Chad, Chad, do I have a cigarette in my hand?"

Chad said, "No."

My dad heard "Chad" and "cigarette," and he leaped out of that chair! He snatched Chad around and said, "Don't you dare give him a cigarette, boy!"

I told Chad, "I guess I was dreaming, and boy, it was good." There is no doubt in my mind that if Dad had not been there and I wanted a cigarette, Chad would have given me one. He was awesome. He passed away October 23, 2009, while I was having surgery in San Antonio. I could not go to the hospital or the funeral, but I did ask one of my pastors, Lee Yancy, to go. Lee was also a state senator. He prayed with

Chad and was there for his family. Thanks, Lee! I am grateful for the memories Chad and I made.

In the meantime, Chad and my daddy came together to visit me on alternating weekends. A cousin, Billy Lee, came on the weekends Dad and Chad didn't come. I would not let Billy leave until the NASCAR race was over on Sundays. I was so blessed to have him there. He did things just like A'Leta, things the doctors and nurses didn't want to do. He did everything—from helping me go to the bathroom to holding me when I cried. He even cut up my food.

I hated being alone. A'Leta was staying in town at a hotel. She would tell me she'd be back soon, but the hours and occasionally days she needed to be away seemed like an eternity to me. She had to take time for herself and for Carney. I got weepy, sure that she'd never come back, that she was sick of me, and that she had a new boyfriend. My mental state wasn't helped by one of the hospital's counselors, who began to try to prepare me that I should let A'Leta leave me. They said young wives never stay.

"She's young and pretty. She's going to get tired of the stress of all this," she said. "You need to prepare yourself for the day she tells you she's leaving you." She said this is what usually happens in cases of severe trauma like mine. "It might take awhile, but it will happen." She was just trying to get me to be realistic.

I later found an article that describes some of the things I was going through:

> Burn injury may affect all aspects of human life, leaving survivors with a variety of physical and psychosocial handicaps. In addition, altered appearance and stigmatization may represent a threat to patient's social life. Burn survivors often have a challenging and protracted recovery process. Somatic symptoms are generally persistent and psychiatric disorders such as post-traumatic stress disorders (PTSD) and depression are relatively frequent.[24]

All these issues affected my outlook. I didn't see what my face looked like until three weeks before I went into rehab.

A'Leta says today, "All burn patients look alike." She doesn't mean that in a harsh way. She's just stating the truth. Reconstruction, including facial reconstruction, has to follow specific paths. Burn survivors need a nose. They need eyelids. They need a mouth. There is only so much a plastic surgeon can do in those initial months to individualize a person's looks. The first work at hand is to give the person the physical characteristics that make the person look human, not specifically like the person used to look.

I knew this, and yet … when a nurse finally handed me a small, round mirror, I looked at the mask of a face looking back at me. I couldn't get my mind around what I was looking at. It wasn't me. The eyes and the voice were mine, but the image was not me. I saw a monster.

"You turn around and leave me now, and don't ever come back!" I yelled. A'Leta tried to argue with me, but I meant it. I made her leave. For two weeks I didn't want anyone in the room with me.

Bless her heart, Carney was not threatened. She was sitting on my bed and we were coloring one day. I took her hand and said, "Daddy looks different, doesn't he?"

She told me, "Yeah, but you still look real good, Daddy." That sweet answer made me realize I had to put my "big boy britches on" and try to begin to deal with my outward appearance.

Six weeks after I was burned, my ears fell off.

ONWARD TO REHAB

A'Leta

Four and a half months after Jack's injuries, the surgeon reluctantly released him to Methodist Rehab In-patient in Jackson, Mississippi, about twelve miles from our home. We had him moved there by ambulance. It had gotten to the point where Carney cried the entire time I was away from her. I didn't think our little girl could take one more day of being separated from us. Because of that, I pushed for him to be transferred.

I learned right away why the doctor had not wanted to send him to rehab yet. The staff there would not touch Jack. They freaked out. They acted clueless about what to do, but I think the real reason they wouldn't touch him is that they didn't want to do his dressing changes. They had never seen or experienced burns of this magnitude.

In a rehabilitation center, a patient gets a lot—and I do mean a lot—less care than he does in the hospital. Dressing changes were not part of the daily routine here. The focus is on therapy: physical, speech, and occupational.

So, I did Jack's dressing changes. The first one took me four hours. Four hours of him squalling in pain. It took me awhile because I didn't really have a lot of stuff. I was just trying to do whatever to get through that morning. After the first few days, it got better. Nobody there ever helped me—not one time—except for Bruce, one of the nurses. After Carney started school and I had to be home to see her off, Bruce would start on him. By the time I arrived, he'd have most of the old bandages off, and maybe even have him showered. Then I could pick up where he left off. I would give him his bath and bandage him up. When I say "bandage," I don't mean "a Band-Aid here and a Band-Aid there." I mean bandages from his head, face—everything—to his toes.

Jack got a staph infection after we moved him to rehab, so his entire face had to be bandaged. His skin looked like raw hamburger meat from head to toe. It was that bad. Blood was still pouring out from everywhere, even after four months and seventeen days in the hospital. Counting back, I now realize he had open wounds in one place or another for a year and a half.

We got through the dressing changes. After the first few days, it got to the point where I was moving fast, trying to get the dressings changed as fast as I could. The quicker I could get it done, the less time he had to hurt. My dad came in to help me in the mornings. He started a pattern of coming in to help me regularly until Jack was released. My brother-in-law, Scott Hickman, worked at the VA hospital next door to the rehab center. If he worked the night shift, he would come in and help me do dressing changes at 7:00 a.m. when he got off, in order to give my dad a break. Between Scott and Daddy, they helped me get through what was a time-consuming and very emotional process for me, and a painful for one for Jack.

God also gave me the ability to step aside emotionally and treat Jack like a regular patient, and not like a family member. Like a nurse who does this kind of thing every day, I did what I had to do and moved on to the next thing. I learned to tune out Jack's crying. He'd be squalling, but there was nothing I could do for him except to move faster. The more he cried, the faster I worked. If I could just get through it, it would quit hurting him so much.

At first, Bruce, the nurse, came into the room in the middle of what I was doing, to try to calm Jack down a little. After about a week, we got the procedure timed to where Bruce would come in and give Jack his first shot of pain meds. Then, after I'd been working on Jack for about an hour, he returned and gave him another shot. That would get him through the rest of dressing changes.

Jack spent a long six weeks in Methodist Rehab. During those weeks, I went home at night to be with Carney, and I stayed with Jack during the day. When we were in Shreveport, Louisiana, H&P had booked me a two-bedroom suite at the Ramada from the beginning. This was a huge blessing because I didn't have to worry about cleaning, and I had a place where my mama or whoever else was visiting could stay. The company was great to us during the whole time … though I know it was the least they could do.

Jack was anxious to get home. I was too, since it would mean we could be together again and with Carney. Coming to rehab was hard on my dad and my brother-in-law, and on our pastor and our faithful friends as well, who kept supporting Jack and me with their visits.

It was time to go home, but I didn't have a clear understanding of how hard this would be.

HOME, SWEET RETROFITTED, HOME

A'Leta

The doctor told me at the beginning of Jack's stay in rehab that he would probably be there for four weeks. We didn't find out until the third or fourth week that we had to have our whole bathroom remodeled so I could bring him home. That prolonged his stay at rehab. The shower had to be redone so he could get in and out easily. The sink had to be changed so he could get a wheelchair under it.

I asked the guys to put a huge TV in the bathroom during the remodeling because that was where I would do his dressing changes. I hoped that Jack would be able to lie down and watch the TV; maybe it would distract him from the pain a little bit. There were a lot of other little things that needed changing too, like the way doors opened, and the ramps that needed to be built on the outside of the house.

Our house was very open, so it was pretty easy to adapt to the situation. When Jack entered Methodist Rehab, I gave the staff a list of the supplies I would need for dressing changes once Jack got home.

Jack came home in August 2006, more than six months since that horrific night on March 3. After we got him in the house and situated in his room, I took care of him. I didn't have home health care yet. The visiting nurses started coming the next week, but having them there was often more trouble than it was worth. They didn't know what to do. I had to tell them, and Jack wouldn't let anybody but me touch him, anyway. They couldn't do his dressing changes, so they just stood there and handed me supplies. We had a few good nurses who helped out, but there were days at first when I didn't even have a bath. Jack's needs were constant.

Here is a typical day during those first few weeks: I got up early to get Carney ready and drive her to school, leaving Jack in bed. When I came home, I cooked him a full breakfast. He was supposed to have 3,000 calories a day, so the big breakfast got him off to a good start. I went into the bedroom, pulled him out of bed, helped him sit carefully in his wheelchair, and got him to his food. He ate, and then we did dressing changes.

I gloved and gowned up to start the grueling process of changing the dressings. I need to describe the way Jack's skin looked. His legs were a mottled, angry, bruised-looking combination of nearly every shade of red or dark pink I can name—maroon, magenta, mauve, reddish-gray, as well as plain red and bright pink.

First, I cut off the bandages as he sat in a chair. Then I helped him gently but quickly pull off his shirt so I could get to the gauze wrapped around his torso. I cut them off with razor blades very carefully so as not to disturb the skin that had closed up and was not bleeding any longer. I cut off his arm bandages in the same way I had removed the leg ones. On his arms and legs were sores and scabs that were still oozing large amounts of drainage, even after all the time he had spent in medical facilities.

When I finished his arms, Jack got a handheld shower going. He was able to use it a little. I finished what he was not able to do for himself. After that, I helped him lie down and rubbed medication into each limb. Then I wrapped each limb with several layers of medicated gauze—round and round, round and round. These processes went more quickly when I had someone to help, but often I did them alone.

We gently rolled protective sleeves called Tubigrip on his arms and legs, then I cleaned out and changed his trache. I helped him sit up and placed medicated gauze where he needed them on his back and shoulders before winding gauze around his torso. I stretched an undershirt over the bandages, then a shirt over that, and finally helped him put on some loose-fitting pants.

By the time I finished all of that, it was mid-morning. I had to wash the sheets every day, sometimes two or even three times a day, because he bled so much. I was washing constantly—laundry out the wazoo—washing around the clock. I took Jack to outpatient therapy everyday for two hours. Then it was time to cook his lunch. I got his lunch done, and then it was something else and something else, until it was time to pick Carney up from school.

Bless her heart … Carney was home with us, but she had to fend for herself. I couldn't do anything with her because I had to tend Jack 24/7. I fed Carney her supper, but as far as having interaction time with her, I didn't. What time she had with us was helping me take care of her daddy.

I realize now that Jack came home too soon. Dr. Sittig had tried to persuade me to be realistic about what was ahead. "I'm concerned that you won't be able to handle all the things Jack will need done," he had said.

"I've gotta get him home," I'd insisted. "I've gotta handle this. I don't have a choice. Carney will be starting school soon, and I've got to be there." Then I'd told Jack, "If you don't go home, that's fine, but you're gonna be here by yourself during the week. I will go home during the week so I can be there for Carney for school, and then she and I will come on the weekends." Those first few weeks, I think I performed once again as a sort of robot. One of my entries describes how I was managing:

September 16, 2006

> Jack, Mom, and I went shopping yesterday to look for some pants for Jack and to get out of the house. You did great, Jack, but when we got home, I fell apart. I would for once like to come in the house and just take a bath or shower and go to bed. I do not even know who I am anymore, because I have no emotions or feelings unless it is about Jack. I am very tired and give out. I would love to

have my own life again. I know that this is God's will, but I am still human.

We had our up days, and we had our down days. September 25, about a month after we got home, we had an up day. I wrote, "You are doing better mentally … and every day is getting better … I feel that maybe one day we may actually resume a more normal life."

Not so fast, though. The next day I wrote,

September 26, 2006

We are not having a good day today. I think that we are sick of each other, considering we have never spent this much time together. You do not realize how demanding you are being, and I am sure you think that I do not realize how confrontational I am being. I do not have anybody to express my feelings to, and you are it. I am sorry for that but at this point in my life I do not have a social life, a job, or an identity of my own, and I am having a hard time adjusting to our new normal. I do love you and I would like for us to be able to enjoy this time that we have together.

Even though we do not recognize it, these moments are truly a blessing from God. We had been saying before you got hurt that we wished we had more time together as a family. I know this is not exactly what we had in mind, but I guess it is what God had in mind. My mama always told me that God had a sense of humor. I sure hope he is laughing, because I don't think it is very funny right now. Maybe I will one day!

We went to church together for the first time on September 27. I noted, "Jack did okay … He did get a little nervous a couple of times. Everyone was so thrilled to see us. Our church family has been such a blessing during this time. Having them has made this ordeal much easier."

As I've already said, we thank God for these people. We have hundreds of e-mails from them, and many made the long trek from the Florence/Jackson area to visit us in Shreveport. After we got back to our home in Florence, Mississippi, they brought meals, and sent cards.

A few of the men came and played dominoes with Jack. That was so special for Jack!

Jack

I had been to hell and back, as we say in the South. But I had no idea what hell was really like until Methodist Rehab released me so I could go home.

A'Leta was in charge of the bathroom remodel. Her friend Kelly's dad, Mr. Powell, had come and done all the construction, with the cost covered by Worker's Comp. He and his men redid the shower so I could use it. What they didn't ask was, *How am I going to be able to do that?* A'Leta had to become my 24/7 nurse.

The first morning, my dressing change took her six hours. That was the first time I stood for a minute in front of a full-length mirror. I almost fainted when I saw myself.

I couldn't do anything at home, inside or outside. When I went to the bathroom, I still had to use my left hand. It was impossible to totally manage my personal needs. It was awhile before I could go to the bathroom entirely by myself. That first day I was able to take care of my own needs, I got a feeling of freedom that is hard to describe. Think of what it would be like not to be able to do this most basic human thing by yourself, but having to let someone else do it for you. All my dignity was gone.

That's what A'Leta did for me. And she didn't complain. She just did it. I finally got to where I could wipe, and then I had to use my left hand. Let me tell you, it sounds funny now, but when you are right-handed and you have to use your left hand, you will chase yourself all around the bathroom trying to catch your rear end.

Meanwhile, I had to adjust to Carney's confusion about how to act around her daddy with all the hard-to-accept changes, not only in my looks but in my strength and abilities to be the strong protector and fix-it man she had had before March 2006. Carney had been without a mom or dad at home for more than six months. I know she was glad to have me home, but she said something to me that was hard to hear: "Daddy, please don't come into my bedroom at night, okay?"

"Why, baby?"

"You scare me."

Most of the time at home Carney didn't seem to hesitate being close to me. She even had a protective attitude toward me. But she told A'Leta she didn't want to go anywhere out in public with me, not to the store or anywhere (not that I was able or ready to go yet). "I can't stand it if anyone makes fun of Daddy," she said. That was hard.

There were times when I was so down and depressed that A'Leta finally got all my guns out of the house. She was worried I might kill myself, and I would have if it had been easy to do.

These were the days when I came to know something of the pain of Jesus. I thought of him, probably nude, hanging in the heat, skin tearing. I understood a little about that pain. Sometimes when I was being stretched, my skin would tear. When I did rehab at home, my bandages rubbed against my legs and hurt them so much that I had to do the exercises in the nude. I had been told at the Center that pressure releases on my skin would help me feel better, so A'Leta and I tried to find a massage therapist to work with me.

No surprise—they all refused, until we found the Therapeutic Touch Clinic in Flowood, Mississippi, and Miss Barbara. One massage of hers did as much for me as a week of rehab. Starting out, it was just pressure. She then moved to small amounts of rubbing and light pressure. Eventually, it made my skin somewhat soft and pliable, even though the massages hurt badly.

At times, though, in spite of her carefulness, my skin would tear. Once, after a hard day of rehab and massage therapy, my skin became hot. I asked Dr. Sittig's staff at LSU if they knew why this would happen. They thought I might have a blood clot. "You need to come in and be checked for this," they told me.

It turned out that my body could not flush out the amount of toxins being released. When you have a massage or a workout, the muscles release toxins; however, my body was unable to flush them out. The toxins my muscles released had caused a massive infection. I also remember it happened in my right leg. We got it cleared up, only to have the infection return.

I was in a wheelchair much of the time, but slowly I began to walk. Later, we bought a Chevy Tahoe with leather seats. I had to have the leather so I could slide in and out easier. If I tried to slide over cloth, my skin rolled up and it hurt too much. With the Tahoe, A'Leta could drive and I could go more easily to physical therapy three times a week, doctors' appointments, and other places I needed to go.

I continued taking one small step forward at a time, but sometimes it also meant taking a step backwards. A'Leta kept a copy of the newspaper article a reporter wrote about me for the local *Clarion Ledger's* Sunday paper during those first weeks home. That was a bright spot for me, because it allowed me to express how I wanted to use my story for God's glory.

Soon after we got home, it became clear that we might have to move someplace where I could catch my breath easier. The Mississippi heat and humidity made it nearly impossible for me to have any kind of quality of life. I had no sweat glands left, so I couldn't sweat. I could not regulate or release heat. I would dehydrate quickly when I got hot. I also had a hard time breathing in the humidity and heat.

Thankfully, my lungs hadn't sustained much damage, but my rebuilt nose wasn't totally efficient. The climate was also hard on my thin, healing skin. The last thing I needed was the sun blistering my new skin. It had happened a few times, and it happened fast—even through a window. We realized the Jackson area was probably not going to work long-term. But a move, especially one as complicated as mine, would cost money and take lots of prayer.

We both needed to focus on the future. Unfortunately, "future" was another word for "lawsuit," which would be an unpleasant and possibly long, drawn-out process. Thank God for my cousin Chris and our pastor, Lee Yancey. It would take awhile for the lawsuit to go to court, but during the months ahead, they went to bat for us.

CARNEY AND HER DADDY: A'LETA'S JOURNALS

A'Leta

Carney had turned seven years old by the time we finally got home and united as a family. My journal entries not only keep an account of Jack's ongoing surgeries and his first tentative visits into the world outside our house, but they also describe the challenges Carney faced better than any summary I can write.

Thursday, October 19, 2006

This week has been a hard week for me emotionally. Carney has been sick since last Thursday night, and our doctor said he is sure she is having anxiety attacks. She has been vomiting a lot. Workers' Comp is no longer providing a counselor for her, so I am in the process of finding out which one in town will be the best for her and praying about it so that she can get the help she needs.

I went to Hello Beautiful today [the salon shop I owned with Shelley, my lifelong best friend before all this happened] to get a pedicure. That is one of the hardest things for me to do, to go in there and relax. I go in there and sit in the new pedicure chair that I bought and paid for, and I see my new nail table and it is extremely hard ...

I am very concerned about Carney and her well-being. My nerves are starting to bother me, and every time that I eat, I get sick. This has just been one of those weeks, but then again, I cannot even remember my life without one of these weeks. My family has been through so much, and we still have so far to go. I pray constantly for Jack's healing, Carney's healing, my strength, our financial future, and the unknowns ahead. I know that God will take care of all of this but I am still human and think a lot about things. I know that I cannot change any of this or a big part of this, so I am sure that God will handle this.

Friday, October 20, 2006

Jack went to the guest bedroom last night to sleep because Carney was being loud and would not go to sleep. She is not minding and is back-talking every breath. It does not matter how much we correct her, it only gets worse. I know that she is acting out—she has no other way to act. She starts squalling over every little thing, especially if Jack is the one correcting her. I had a meeting with her school counselor yesterday. She is going to talk to her a little bit and start developing a relationship with her so that Carney can talk to her and open up to her if she needs to. I am going to get a referral from our doctor to a psychologist for her who will take our insurance. I do not like feeling this way when it comes to my child. All I want to do is to protect her and make everything perfect for her, but I know that I cannot. She will still not eat with us at the table. She will not eat with Jack or allow him to go anywhere outside of this house with her. It is very hard on him. I know that it is hard on Carney too, because she had a very close relationship with him before this. I know that she is starving for that kind of attention from him and that safety with him, and it kills me to see the both of them hurting for the same things.

Seeing this makes me sick inside and I do not want to eat. When I do eat, I get sick. I cannot be comfortable with the fact of my child being put on a sedative just so that she can make it through the night without throwing up. This makes me feel like I have failed as a parent.

I know that God will heal the scars and wounds Carney has from this. They will never go away completely, but with prayer God can certainly make it easier to live with them and to be able to talk about and to share with other people in the future.

Today is one of those days when I just want to cry. I want my life back and my family back. I know that when I wake up tomorrow it will be better and I will have to pray in the meantime for renewed strength, physically and mentally. I love you, Jack, and I want you to know that when you are reading all of this one day, that I am sorry if I let you or Carney down, and I hope that because of what we have to go through that I can be a better wife and mother. Thank you for being patient with me and loving me no matter what kind of day I am having. Thank you, and I love you with all of my heart.

Sunday, October 29, 2006

We went to Carney's school yesterday to watch her dance. This is the first time Jack has been anywhere in public with her besides church. She did not want him to go, but she did okay. We were there a couple of hours, and he got sunburned on his face and the back of his neck. He has been complaining that it is sore today. His skin is so sensitive, and so far it has never been exposed to anything. Almost every inch of his body is new skin. There are a lot of things that have to take place during the healing process of his skin, and it is an extremely slow process that will take many, many years. There is a good chance that we will be dealing with surgeries and reconstruction for the rest of his life. There again, God is in control, and he will give us the strength to handle whatever comes our way.

Wednesday, November 8, 2006

Yesterday, we went to Carney's school so that Jack could talk to her class about fire prevention and so that the kids could see him and ask questions about his burns. Carney has not wanted him to go in public with her, so the teacher suggested that he come and talk to the class so that Carney could overcome that. Her teacher told us Carney had been so excited about her daddy coming to school. I hope this will help her to understand that just because people look different it is okay. I love her more than anything in this world, and it hurts me terribly to see her feel so torn up inside and have such confusion about what is going on with her life.

Jack has had a very tiring week. I think he is just physically exhausted from therapy this week. He gets a little better and his skin is doing well, but we get one place cleared up and another place starts to open up. Then we have to start all over.

Monday, December 13, 2006

... All of this stress overflows into Carney's already hard and difficult life. My seven-year-old has been through more in the past nine months than most will ever have to go through in a lifetime. When it comes to having to settle with all [the people involved in causing Jack's injuries or in the calculation of his benefits], no dollar amount can replace our lives. I pray that God will bless us with every penny that these companies have, and more. I pray that God will change my heart and help me forgive, as well.

Wednesday, December 29, 2006

Jack's surgeries and treatments are moving really fast. It is good but also tiring and stressful for both of us and the rest of the family. My dad always goes with us. There's the stress [for my mom] of Carney squalling for days before we go and then her giving her Nana hell while we are gone. She does not do well and is scared that we are not going to come home. Dr. Bishop has put her on a new antidepressant in the past couple of weeks. She is doing great with it, but I have issues with my seven-year-old being on an antidepressant. He thinks she can stop taking it once she gets over this hump. I am proud of her, and it hurts when I think about what could possibly be going on inside of her.

Monday, January 21, 2007

Today Jack spoke at Briar Hill Nursing Home and did a great job. He was released to drive this week and has driven a little bit. He is only driving around the community until he gets comfortable with it. I am proud of him, but it seems that the better he gets the worse Carney gets.

We are having a time with her and her behavior. I know that God will heal her, but I am sure that it will take time. I have sat and cried because I have no idea how to help her deal with everything going on.

We have to go to Shreveport next week for a doctor's appointment. Jack is having steroid injections in the scar tissue around his mouth to try to loosen up the scar tissue. He will also see the hand surgeon and have some tests done. It will be very tiring on him and me.

There again, God will give us the strength to make it. I long for the family bond that we all three had before this tragedy. I feel like I am just surviving, and my brain cannot even begin to think about tomorrow or any future *anything* as far as our family is concerned. Our whole life is based on doctor's appointments, surgeries, therapy, and Carney's school activities, and that is it.

Thursday, February 1, 2007

Monday, January 29, we went to the hand surgeon so she could check Jack's hand again. We got great news—she said the nerve was intact and regenerating itself, and he should have full function in his right hand in three to four months.

That is great! I remember the conversation with Dr. Sittig, when he predicted that Jack would lose all of his fingers and parts of his hands and I told him no, he would not. My God will heal them completely, and he is. When Dr. Sittig told me what he did, I prayed that if God was not going to heal his hands, then to please go ahead and take him home. I did not want him to have to live not being able to feel me or to brush Carney's hair.

God is so good, and he blesses us with many blessings each and every day. I am proud of how faithful Jack is to the Lord. It would be just as easy for him to be angry or question, "Why me?" Instead, he is trying to make the best of what God has given him and using it to help other people.

God is opening doors for Jack to speak and to share his story, and he will continue to open doors for our family. Carney is doing some better. We are going to a new psychologist and we like her. We are all in agreement that something has to be done right away to get her under control. The psychologist said that if Carney is not better by summer we will have to consider inpatient treatment, which I am totally against. We have also decided to put her in private school next year, which we cannot afford, but we believe that it will be best for her. It is very structured Christian school, and she will learn self-control and be better prepared to cope.

The psychologist said Carney was forced into an adult situation before she was able to become mature and handle it—which we already knew—but we did not know how to help her get through this in the most effective way. She is so precious. God has plans that we do not even know yet. This might be to make her readily able to work with other people going through similar tragedies.

Sunday, March 11, 2007

Today Jack had to be admitted to LSU for his neck release tomorrow morning.[25] He is scared and upset. I am unable to stay with him because I have Carney, and my dad will not be here until late tonight. It bothers me that I cannot be with him because I feel like he needs me right now. We cannot leave Carney here with my mom because she cries from severe separation anxiety. I hope and pray that Jack will be okay tonight. I will be there early in the morning to see him before he goes to surgery. I have been there every step of the way, and this is the first time I have been unable to be right there with him. God will take care of everything just like he always does.

Saturday, April 14, 2007

Jack was supposed to have surgery on April 11, but he has had an allergic reaction to one of the antibiotics they gave him. He was swollen and blood-red. Later in the day, his hand started splitting open and fluid was coming out. He was miserable. He had to have steroids, Benadryl, and more antibiotics.

Dr. Sittig did his surgery the next day, which was April 12. He took a very large piece of skin from his stomach and put a graft on his neck. Jack did really well in surgery and after. This is the first time he has not cried and gone psycho on me.

We came home yesterday, April 13, with a shot of Fentanyl[26] as we were leaving the hospital. On the way home, he started crying and did not do well. The ride made him start hurting. I had to stop several times and readjust his bandages and how he was sitting. I gave him several morphine tabs on the way home and none of that worked. Today he has done much better. He did not sleep last night, so he has rested a lot today.

Carney was very mad at us when we got home because she did not get to go with us. She was upset and crying, so my dad had to come get her yesterday evening because Jack could not handle her screaming. I pray that she will get better.

Friday, November 9, 2007

Jack had a surgery today, and the surgery went well. He had a second neck release.[27] It was cut from one side of his neck to the other in the front, with the cut left open about four inches. They put faux skin on, and in four weeks they will graft it. They stapled it and stitched a bolster on it all the way around. The pain is excruciating and nothing is helping. He cannot really move because when he does, it pulls his skin where the bolster is stitched to his neck all the way around the cut. It is just miserable, and there is nothing I can do to ease the pain. Instead of getting easier every time we do this, it gets harder and harder.

Carney is not doing well emotionally. She finally told me the other day that the way her daddy looked before and a lot of the times that they spent together are gone from her memory. The only thing she has is pictures. That kills me more than anything so far. It feels like my insides and my soul have been ripped out and there is no way I will ever get them back. I can't imagine not having the memories of my own daddy, the one man that I have been in love with since birth and will always be in love with until death. I think of her one day telling her kids and grandchildren about her daddy, when all she'll remember before she was six years old is vague and what she has been told by others. I can't begin to understand her feelings. All I know is that from a mother's standpoint it hurts beyond what words can express, and it stirs anger and every other emotion that a person can possibly have. Then, there is the way Jack would feel if he knew this, but I think that it is something he does not need to hear right now. He has a hard enough time as it is. I just continue to pray. I know that God is in control and he will always work it out for the good of his children. "We know that all things work together for the good of those who love God: those who are called according to His purpose" (Rom. 8:28 HCSB).

Sunday, December 1, 2007

Carney and I are having another Christmas season with you [Jack], and it is wonderful. She seems to be doing better with you this week. Monday she slept with you in your chair for a couple of hours because neither one of you could sleep and she seems to be talking more respectfully this week.

This Christmas is better than last year, but I also think back to Christmas 2005 when things were perfect. You worked on Christmas, and we had Christmas as a family before you left. You gave my daddy a copperpearl bracelet to match the copper coin pearl necklace that you had given me before you left so that I would have something to open on Christmas. Of course, my daddy couldn't find the package with the bracelet in it and that was a circus, but it wouldn't be Christmas without a Combs family moment.

I asked Carney on the way to the school Tuesday morning if she liked snuggling with Daddy, and she smiled and said yes. I said, "It feels pretty good, doesn't it?" and she said yes. I said, "He is still the same daddy inside." She said, "I know." I hope now that she feels safe with you again that she will crave more and more of you. I hope that one day she can enjoy the fact that God let you stay here with us.

This week we are going to be getting ready to go back to Shreveport for another surgery. I have not even thought about what we are going to do about Carney, because she freaks out. I know that I have to face it, but things have been so good this week that I know this is will be a major setback for her and for us.

Sunday, December 2, 2007

This week I will be getting all of our stuff ready to go to Shreveport. Jack has a surgery scheduled for Friday, December 7. He will be having the graft done on his neck. Carney will go to my sister's, but she does not know, and we are not going to tell her. My sister will pick her up from school on Thursday, and maybe Carney will not panic. I hope this surgery goes well, and I hope Carney is going to be okay. I hope that one day she can forgive me and her daddy for the hard life that she is having to live. Jack and I are her protection and safety, and she looks to us to protect her from the exact thing that is happening to her. Inconsistency, not knowing, and not understanding anything about our life now is what has turned her once perfect and carefree world into fear and sadness. It kills me, and I have to pray, and I know that God is using this to mold her into what she will become for him one day. He is also changing Jack and me to become what he wants us to be for him. I have to pray daily that he will continue to give me the faith I need to withstand whatever it is he has in store for us.

Friday, December 7, 2007

Jack had a surgery today on his neck again. Dr. Sittig grafted it where he had cut it open four weeks ago. Surgery went great, but after he got back in the room, he started having chest pain and heaviness, sweating, and shortness of breath, and he started vomiting. They did an EKG, chest X-ray, and blood work. They could not find anything. It was scary for me and Jack. They even went and got Dr. Sittig out of the operating room to come down there. They had all the doctors, nurses, respiratory therapists, and anesthesiologists in there, trying to figure out what was going on.

All I could do was hold Jack's hand and be there for him. I just prayed and prayed. This has not happened before, and it was not a very good feeling for either one of us. I knew that when Dr. Sittig came out of the OR to see him, there was a potential problem. I thank God that everything turned out okay. Even though he has come this far, each time he goes into surgery he is at great risk of complications and/or death.

Carney is staying with my sister and my mom. She does not even know we are here, because she panics and cries for the entire time we are gone. She does not need to miss school. They are telling her that Jack and I and my dad are doing Christmas shopping and trying to get all that done. My dad comes with me so that he can help me drive and help me with Jack. Daddy got very scared today and left the room. He was out in the hall, and I think he was crying, or about to. We are all trying our best to accept that this is our life now and that we will never be normal again.

We have to come back next week for a check-up and appointment with a plastic surgeon. We will have to bring Carney, because we will not be able to get by with this again. I will stay with Jack tonight to make sure he is going to be okay and does not have any more problems. We will go home on Sunday because I have taken him home in the past the day of or the day after surgery. The trip and ride are very hard on him, my dad, and me. Maybe by staying in the hospital until Sunday, the ride will not be as bad. The donor site is on his stomach and it will stay sore for weeks, so I do not know if it will be much better or not. I pray that it is.

Jack comments about that December …

In spite of the surgery, I enjoyed that Christmas season. My growing-up years didn't hold good memories of Christmas. Before the accident that time was even a little depressing for me. My memories were tangled up with the sadness I felt as a kid because my family was not together. Before I got hurt on the rig, it was a little depressing for me as well, and I always had to work Christmas Day and be away from A'Leta and Carney.

Christmas 2007 was different. Carney wanted to sit on my lap. The feelings I got from that were as fresh and new as the feelings I'd had the first time I ever held her after she was born. And then, because *she* wanted to sit on my lap, our little nieces Kameron and Ella Riley, Tu's little girls, wanted to get in on the action. They were only about three and four at the time, and they wanted to be with Uncle Jack.

I was beginning to get little glimpses of something else too. A'Leta and I were transitioning. There were moments when we could feel "married." We could feel like a husband and wife again—not like a patient and caregiver. For a little while, we both could see little patches of light.

A'Leta reminded me of something Kameron had been doing at preschool that fall. When the kids colored, she would draw pictures of a man on fire. The teacher, who knew about us but didn't know Kameron was related to us, was worried about the drawings. As soon as my sister-in-law Brooke told the teacher I was Kameron's uncle, she quit worrying. "No need to explain," she told Brooke. Though Ella Riley was too young to understand everything, Kameron always has been, and still is, unusually sensitive to others' pain.

Thursday, January 10, 2008

Today Jack was scheduled for liposuction,[28] fat transplants, and removal of the trache. This was supposed to be his last surgery for a while. Dr. Sittig wants him to take a couple of years off to let his body heal and try to recover from the shock of so many surgeries in a short period of time. God is great, and I know that he knows what's best because the surgery was cancelled at the last minute. His IV was in and he was in the OR, when all the surgeries had to be cancelled because the city had a water main break and there was no water pressure. He and Carney were so excited because he would be getting the trache out. This was a mental blow to him and Carney both. It is hard for all of us because this was a huge deal for Jack, and he has been looking forward to this for a year or more.

God has a plan, and I trust his will. I pray that he will comfort Jack and Carney both. I know that he will. His surgery is scheduled for January 24. I am very tired because I drove to Shreveport yesterday, and we sat in the doctor's office for four and a half hours. Today we got up at 5:30 a.m. We did not leave the hospital until 11:00 a.m. and then I drove home.

I think that I am so tired mentally and physically that the surgery being cancelled did not have much of an effect on me. My mind and body are on the bottom, and at this point I have to go up. I have been saying this for almost two years, and I am still the same. Right now, as long as I can keep Jack and Carney mentally sane then I am okay. I can find sanity at a later date and time. God keeps refilling me because that is the only way that I can keep going day after day with no time at all for myself.

A'Leta

During this time, we were having big issues with the nurses and other caregivers being paid by Workers' Comp to help me care for Jack as well as with the case worker who was supposed to be with us during surgeries and be our advocate in many ways. Neither arrangement was working well, and we were left many times not knowing what to do or what the next step was. Meanwhile, Carney continued to suffer from abandonment and anxiety. She needed therapy—but again, fighting red tape was a major headache in order to get it for her.

Thursday, January 17, 2007

Jack's surgery is scheduled for January 24. Since it was cancelled last week, things have been a little tense. We had to come home and tell Carney that Daddy did not get his trache out and let her down again. I feel like she is accustomed to being disappointed. I hate that my baby cannot have even a partially normal existence, because she is crying out for her daddy and me. She wants and needs attention that sometimes it is not possible for us to give her. Jack needs a lot of sleep and by the time Carney gets out of school in the afternoons, he is really tired. I stay exhausted and feel guilty for not making myself do more with her. I am often at the breaking point when the time comes to be able to be the mother to her that she needs. I have to pray daily for strength and for God to overflow me with his love so that I can pour out that same kind of love to Carney and Jack. I am torn, weak, and broken. Only God can sustain me on a daily basis.

Saturday, February 2, 2008

Jack had lipo, fat injections, and the trache taken out January 24. He was in a lot of pain and had trouble right after surgery. Carney cried the three days we were gone. She finally told my mom that she thought her daddy was gonna die in surgery. It gets harder for her every time we leave, instead of easier. Her grades the week of his surgery were very bad. Her teacher understands why and she works with her and is not concerned that much about it. Hopefully, Jack will not have to have any more surgeries for a while. Dr. Sittig thinks he needs to take a break and let his body heal and recoup from all the trauma and all the surgeries in a short period of time. Maybe we can all rest and try to recoup somewhat. God will take care of us no matter what, and I still have the faith in him that sustains me from day to day. He provides me strength beyond my understanding and beyond the understanding of the people around me. I hope that I can be a witness and an example for other women who may be experiencing similar situations.

Monday, June 16, 2008

Yesterday, Carney and I gave Jack the scrapbook that I have been working on for about a year and a half. Since Jack got hurt, Carney has been through hell, and we have no way of understanding what she goes through on a daily basis, emotionally and socially. Well, yesterday she decided that she is going to be her daddy's little shadow again. She actually got up in the chair with him, kissed him about every five minutes, and told him she loved him very, very much with all her heart, mind, and soul.

I can honestly say that yesterday was the best day of Jack's life since March 3, 2006. Today she did the same thing. I am praying that this continues, because for her to go back now would be devastating for Jack. He is eating her up and enjoying every minute of it. This is an answer to the prayer we have been praying since he was hurt. I have the faith that God has answered this prayer just like so many others that we pray every day.

Monday, September 15, 2008

Carney is still having extreme ups and downs in dealing with Jack and the tragedy of our family. We are consistently praying and trusting in God to heal her of the emotional scars in her life that are making it hard for her to function day to day. It is so hard for me as a mom to sit back and not be able to do anything about it except to love her, and that is just not enough most of the time. I am so ready to move on, and I have to deal with the fact that there is no moving on. This is our life and it is here to stay. Some days I look back and think that we have come so far, and then there are those days when I wake up and I feel like I cannot see light at the end of the tunnel. I guess this is all part of this whole process that we are going through, whatever that process may be.

LEE, CHAD, AND A FUNERAL

Jack

By the time A'Leta and I got back in our house in Florence, Mississippi, I had grown to love and appreciate the new pastor of our home church.

Brother Danny visited frequently at the rehab center in Jackson. He came two days a week at about 6:00 a.m.—pretty early for someone who had to drive all that way to see me.

He'd asked me, "What time do you go to rehab?"

"I start around 7:30 and go to about 10:00," I told him.

"If I get here about 6:00, you'll be up?"

"Yeah, I'll be eatin' breakfast." So he came. He left our church eventually, but how much he helped me is impossible for me to even put down on paper.

Lee Yancey became the interim pastor. He and I got along well, and he probably saved my sanity several times. He was able to offer comfort to my family in an unexpected way during my most recent surgery in 2009. I was in San Antonio, having some extensive skin grafting and repair to my right hand. We had to stay there at least six weeks. A'Leta's mother and daddy, bless their hearts, were with us to help out. Our sister-in-law Brooke sent out an update to family and friends, who were awaiting word on how things had gone:

> 12:35 p.m.—Hey, guys! Everyone please keep Billy Jack in your prayers today. He is in surgery now, and the doctors will be doing three major surgeries while he is in there. Please keep him in your prayers and lift A'Leta, Carney, Edra, and Lemuel up as well. They're all there to help care for and comfort Jack during a long recovery, approximately six weeks. God bless and have a great day. Updates on the surgeries will be posted later in the day!
>
> 7:05 p.m.—OK, guys: Surgery went well. I just talked to A'Leta. She said they told her about an hour ago that they were suturing Jack up. She said the doctor accomplished everything except they only got to fix the thumb on the right hand. The little finger and ring finger will require extensive surgery, so they will have to finish it up in about six months. The doctor thinks his thumb will do great, which is most important. Jack is going to ICU tonight, not because there is anything wrong, it's just as a precaution. This is only so he can come out of anesthesia while he is intubated so that in the event there are any complications, they won't have to intubate him later. It is really difficult for them to intubate him because of the trache that he had when he first got injured. It's all basically a precaution so they will not have to trache him again. Thanks, guys, for all your thoughts and prayers, and please continue to keep the whole family in your prayers!

While I was in the hospital, we received terrible news. My step-brother Chad was dying. He had somehow contracted *E. coli*, and they didn't discover it until it was too late. He had been faithful, coming with my dad every other weekend to visit me. I loved Chad, and I was worried about whether he had accepted the Lord.

I asked Lee to visit him. He did. He didn't call Chad first, but I guess he had called the hospital to see what room Chad was in or something. Those nurses were all excited about Lee's visit. He had been elected to the state senate, so he was a local celebrity of sorts. The nurses were cleaning and getting everything ready because a senator was coming! They told me my brother was so proud. He said, "My brother sent that man to see me."

Lee just put it out there to Chad: "Your brother sent me. He wants to know if you're goin' to heaven or hell."

Chad answered him, "Me and God made things right a couple of days ago."

Lee said, "Your brother wants you to know that he loves you."

Chad wasn't a church-goin' guy. He'd give you the shirt off his back, but he drank his beer or whatever, and it was just a way of life. It didn't make him loved any less. Lee spoke at Chad's funeral. My dad called me, crying. He said, "You'll never know how much that man means to us."

BILLS BY THE TRUCKLOAD

A'Leta

When I first called Chris about what had happened to Jack, I wasn't asking for legal advice. The last thing on my mind was money. I had to call Chris because that's what Jack had long ago told me to do. "Chris will take care of everything if something ever happens to me," he'd told me, so that's what I did. I called Chris a day or two after Jack got hurt.

Jack's instructions hit me all of a sudden during those first couple of days at the hospital. "Oh, my gosh!" I said to Shelley and Stephen. "I haven't called Chris! I need to call him."

Chris was expecting my call—word had quickly passed through our families and friends. My daddy had called Jack's mother's house and spoken with Jack's stepdad about the explosion, and he had also called Jack's daddy. Chris knew I'd call when I was ready. After I called, he took care of all the legal issues from that day forward.

While Chris was collecting evidence for the trial, he received some depositions that surprised him. They especially surprised Jack and me. One doctor wrote, "A'Leta could go back to work. There's no reason she can't go back to work." As if! Was that doctor writing about the right person? Who would care for Jack? He sure couldn't care for himself! Who would care for Carney?

Chris was not having that! He had a video made showing Jack's daily routine, starting from the time he pulled himself out of bed in the morning. We called it "A Day in the Life of Billy Jack McDaniel." Chris also enlisted the services of Dr. Steven Wolf to evaluate Jack's present and future condition. Dr. Wolf's deposition offered his professional opinion: not only was I not able to work, with all I had to do for Jack, but that there was no way Jack could work, either. Dr. Wolf was adamant. He didn't fabricate the truth, and the video didn't lie. The evidence was right there in front of anyone who saw it. To this day, I still can't believe any doctor who knew Jack would think he or I could work!

Jack

For Chris McDaniel, who was not only my cousin but who had dealt with the tragic loss of his father, my case was painfully personal. He was determined to hit a home run for us. He filed a lawsuit against Smith International Company, designers of the RCD mechanism, in the 61st District Court in Houston, Texas.

He began the process of discovery by calling the LSUHSC, the Louisiana State University Hospital. When he told the records clerk who he was and what he wanted, she asked, "Which ones would you like?"

"We want all of 'em," Chris told her.

"Okay, but you realize they're gonna need a few truckloads to bring these things to you."

"I don't care. I need every page of them," he answered.

Chris works out of a beautiful, three-story office in downtown Laurel, Mississippi. During the time our case was ongoing (preparing for the actual trial, filing the depositions, and so on took months), you could not walk into any room in that office that didn't have boxes labeled *McDaniel v. Smith.*

Chris is a great attorney. Recently, he was named one of the top fifty lawyers in Mississippi by the *Mississippi Business Journal.* The Laurel *Leader Call* gave him its 2010 Citizen of the Year award. Because of his personal ethics and reputation, Chris would have been a good choice to handle our case even if he wasn't my cousin, but he treated our case as much more than just a job. I don't think any other attorney would have been able to try that case the way he tried it.

After hearing Chris' opening statement and seeing the video, "A Day in the Life," I'm sure some of the jury were already swayed by the time he was finished. He went more than an hour over his allotted time, but no one objected. No one told him to wrap it up. The defense attorneys sat there and said nothing.

We expected the civil trial to last six to eight weeks. It was over on the third day!

JUDGMENT DAY

August 2009

A'Leta

Chris told us before our case went to trial, "You have one chance to get what you're gonna get. Go for it. You have no idea what complications might come up now, soon, or even thirty years from now that he'll need surgery for."

Chris has already been proven right.

The trial ended up being short because Smith's attorneys were quick enough on the draw to see what was happening. They listened to a judge who saw a massive judgment coming down the pike if the trial went on for weeks or months. So, they settled. The onslaught of Chris' powerful opening statement and the weight of my testimony, and that of rig driller Billy Humble, left them no other choice.

The defense lawyers grilled Billy all afternoon on the Monday the trial opened, and then again on Tuesday morning. The lawyers are allotted a certain amount of time for questioning, and they used every minute. During all that time on the stand—four, five, six hours, whatever it was—Billy never wavered. They went into a lot of technical things with him, details about the rig and operations. They tried any way they could to get Billy to say that the boys did something wrong, or the tool pusher did something wrong, or H&P did something wrong. In other words, that any party but Smith itself was negligent or did something wrong. The attorneys tried and tried. They asked him the same question ten different ways, but Billy never faltered, not one time. He had it together. He knew his stuff, and he wouldn't let them trip him up.

The cross-examination was Tuesday before lunch. It went on until the end of Tuesday afternoon. The defense didn't question me, so I only had to answer questions from Chris. He had me talk about everything: our background, our life before the tragedy that had struck us, what I'd been through because of it, and what our life was like since then.

Chris didn't leave anything out. He asked personal things, things you don't want to discuss with anybody, much less in front of a whole courtroom. When he and his team started asking questions about our sex life, it was embarrassing. But I was ready. I didn't have a doubt that I could do it. I didn't *want* to do it, but several days before I testified, I realized this was part of it—I had to testify. This was what God wanted me to do.

So I sucked it up and testified. I had to do whatever I could for my family. Our prayer from day one, no matter how it turned out, no matter what went on in the courtroom, was that God would be seen there. Even if we had to walk out paying Smith for *our* negligence, even if we walked out with nothing at all, God would be glorified, and it would be all about him.

And he was there! God was there. If anybody in that room questioned their relationship with God or even whether there *was* a God, I'm sure that after the trial, as short as it was, they probably got things straight—because it was amazing!

Amazing how? For one thing, God used a small, insignificant delay to bring the trial to a quick close. We knew negotiations had been going on behind the scenes—back and forth, back and forth—but Jack and I weren't paying attention to the rumors we were hearing. We didn't care. We were prepared to take whatever came down. We were prepared to go all the way, let a jury decide the damages, and then appeal if things didn't turn out in our favor. We were prepared, because by that time we weren't worried about it. God would take care of us. We figured that financially we would be fine either way. We were at the end of our savings, and we didn't know how we would pay the truckloads of medical bills. Still, we understood that if that's what God wanted, then that's what we had to do.

Wednesday morning, one of the jurors was late. The two sides were dickering back and forth, waiting for the juror to arrive. The defendants had, from what I could count, about twenty attorneys. They were representing three different companies. The insurance companies involved must have had ten or more attorneys present. I think Chris had five of his team there that day. The judge sent the plaintiff's side (our side) out to come up with a number for a settlement.

Carney and Jack were not in court that morning. Jack was not physically or mentally able to sit in a courtroom all day. He needed to rest, and we felt Carney did not need to be exposed to more trauma than she had already had to experience. The judge had someone call Jack to come over to court from the hotel. Once again, he asked for a dollar figure from us, even though we'd already done this the day before. So, we sent in our number. The defendants' attorneys sent their number in again too.

After we sent our number in, Judge James Wesley[29] called Chris and his team into his chambers. Then he told them they needed to call me.

Chris came into the little room where I was waiting. "The judge is asking for you to come into his chambers," he said.

At first, I just sat there. I wasn't sure Chris was talking to me. I thought he was talking to a couple of his paralegals, who were sitting with me.

Chris pointed at me and said, "He wants *you*, A'Leta."

"Me? Okay. Well, let's go then," I said. "I'm ready."

"No, just hold on a minute. We have to discuss this."

"What's there to discuss?" I asked. "Let's just go. What's he wanna talk about?"

"No, you don't understand."

The paralegals' eyes looked ready to pop out of their heads. They were speechless. The next person slated to testify was sitting there with me too. He was looking at me with an expression that said, "Go, girl, tell him. You go, and you handle it."

Chris said, "First of all, A'Leta, you don't argue with the judge. It doesn't matter what he says, you don't argue. You just say, 'Yes, Your Honor,' and go on."

I think Chris was worried that I might get bossy and tell the judge what was what! "Chris," I said. "I think God has been preparing me for this moment all my life. I'm prepared, or he wouldn't be allowing me to go right now. I'm ready. We're ready."

"Okay, I'm just telling you."

I said, "Let's go and get it done."

We walked in there with four attorneys from our side. The other side's attorneys were still out in the courtroom, conferring about what their next step would be, I guess. They didn't see me go back there. Our attorneys didn't reveal to me right then that a judge calling a plaintiff into his chambers is unheard of.

Right before I went into the room, Chris stopped me. "Now, A'Leta, you don't understand. This has never happened before."

We got back there and walked into his chambers. And God was in that room, the Holy Spirit. I was on holy ground in that judge's chambers. I knew it. I could feel the Lord's presence.

Judge Wesley got up from his desk. He walked over, shook my hand, and introduced himself. "I just wanted to meet you personally. I need to talk to you. I do want you to know that this has never happened in my courtroom before. I would be willin' to bet it's never happened in anybody else's courtroom, either."

He looked at me and continued, "You don't ask the plaintiff back to your chambers and speak to them on a personal basis—*ever.* But I needed to tell you, Mrs. McDaniel, that you are a heroic woman; you are amazing. I had to meet you personally and let you know what an honor it has been serving as judge to you and your family. What you've been through is nothin' like anybody else has ever experienced. Your family's unique. Y'all have been through a tragic event like no other. Nobody else has ever been through anything like this before. And for you to be the way you are, and as strong as you are, and determined as you are, it's phenomenal. I had to meet you in person."

He motioned me to sit down and went back to his desk. "Let's talk about some things," he said and showed me a picture of his boys. "Your daughter is beautiful. My wife would love to have a little girl, one like Carney."

"Yes, Your Honor, she's special," I said.

"I wanted you to know that your testimony has changed my life forever. When I went home yesterday, my kids were outside, playing like they usually play. They were doing nothing unusual, but you know how sometimes you take everyday things like that for granted? If they ask you to do something with them just then you might answer, 'Okay, just give me a minute,' or 'Let's do it in a little bit,' or you kind a brush it off and not think about it again. But yesterday when I came home, one of my sons was waitin' on me out front, excited to show me something new he had learned to do. I thought about how you said your daughter would run out to Jack whenever he walked in the door and jump up in his arms and hug and squeeze him and love him. She lost that. And Jack lost that. I will never take that for granted again."

I answered, "I'm glad. Love your boys. Hug 'em, kiss 'em. Hug your wife. Kiss her, smell her, touch her every chance you have, because you never know. It may not be there tomorrow. It may be taken away. You don't ever want to wish that you could just hug her one more time or kiss her. You never want to regret taking the time to really feel them if they are taken from you for any reason. It's so important. Just the little things that you don't realize are so important."

Then Judge Wesley got down to business. "You sent me your number, and I have the other side's number." He explained about how the jury was going to have to place the blame somewhere. "There's no doubt in my mind that the jury is gonna give you an astronomically large settlement. But you have to remember that it depends on *where* they place that blame as to whether or not you're gonna even get that. You have several defendants out there. One of them's at fault. I have my idea of who it is, but I can't tell you what I think.

"One of them is at fault. The problem is, due to the laws, your employer can't be held responsible if the jury places the blame there. They wouldn't have to pay a thing. They would be off the hook. You would get Workman's Comp, and that would be it.

"You have to keep in mind that we have no way of knowing where the jury is gonna place that blame. Your attorneys are doin' a great job at pointin' the blame to where it needs to be pointed, but at the end of the day, I can't say what a jury is going to decide. But I can tell you, if they *do* put the blame where it needs to go, everybody out there already has their appeal typed up. It'll be in my chambers before they leave here. They will file that appeal, and it can take years and *years*.

"I want your family to be able to pick up the pieces a little bit, to try to move on and get this section of your lives over with. Close this chapter and try to figure out how you're gonna live. And try to get used to this new life. This courtroom is not the place for a ten-year-old. This does not need to be your life.

"I have your two numbers—the number you submitted to me and the number the defendants submitted. I will come up with a number out of these two numbers. If you and Jack will agree to this, they will pay. There won't be any question. They're not gonna make that decision. I'm the judge, and if I say they're gonna pay, they're gonna pay. If you all agree to this, I will make them pay, and this will be over today. I will make them pay and in a timely manner. It will not be drawn out."

"Thank you for that, sir," I said.

He continued. "I'm gonna have a conversation with them. But I can promise you, it's not gonna be anything like my conversation with you. This is my court, and I'm the judge. I can say what's gonna take place, and there's nothin' anybody can say about it."

I said, "Whatever number you decide, we trust you. I'm not worried about that. But I do want you to know that if everything that me and my family have had to go through—if you're the only person it has changed or will ever change, then it's been worth it, and we would do it all over again."

By this point, Judge Wesley was in tears. I was in tears too, and I was feeling the Holy Spirit. He was there, and he was in control of everything. He was directing the judge in what to say. He was telling him, "This is how you're gonna do it."

When we left, Chris said, "I'm so proud of you. You did so good. You didn't jump over the desk or get violent or anything!"

Me? Nah!

When I walked out of his chambers, some of the defense attorneys were standing around in the courtroom. I will *never* forget their faces.

They were in shock. I took my seat, and one of the paralegals or secretaries said, "I've been doin' this for thirty years, and I've never seen this happen before."

By the time I sat down, Jack was there. I could tell he was about to fall off the deep end. I had seen what was happening to Jack emotionally, and I had called Lee, who came from Jackson with one of his comrades, Roger Davis—who works for Woodridge Capital—to be with us in case we had questions. Questions like, "Can I live with this offer? I need to know my bottom dollar, that I can't go any lower."

Jack asked me, "How'd it go?"

"I want you to know, Jack," I told him, "that you have a judge who said he was never gonna mediate, that he doesn't mediate, and he's not gonna *start* mediatin'. But he's mediatin' this case. You get that? He said he was never gonna do it, and he's doin' it. He's adamant about it; he's gonna make it happen today. This is it, Jack. If he comes back with five hundred million dollars or five dollars, that's the number. Whatever he says, that's the number, and we're done."

Judge Wesley sent his number back to us and to the defense. He had a conversation with them, and then he told them that they would be paying the McDaniel Family "X" amount, in "X" amount of time. Everything would be finalized that day, and court would be adjourned.

The judge spoke to the court. It went something like this:[30] "I want everybody to know that everything I did today was for nobody in this room but the McDaniel family. I'm not worried about attorneys, the defendants, or the insurance companies. I don't care. It's about the McDaniel family. It's about their life and their future. I don't care what anybody else thinks.

"About how I made my decision, I'll go ahead and tell you. That way, there'll be no questions as to how I came up with my number. It's customary to take the number from the plaintiff, the number the defendant gives, split it down the middle, and come up with the number. I didn't do that. My number went more towards the side of the McDaniel family. This number will not be published according to the Bluebook,[31] or whatever color book it would be normally published in. It will not be in that. It will not be anywhere. Their names and the amount together will never be public. This family doesn't need that. They need to be able to live a life and not worry about outside influences or anyone from the outside bothering them, hounding them for money. For their protection, this is not gonna be anywhere for anybody to ever see."

Then the judge talked about Carney. "This is not the place for her. I want this to be clear. We will be done with this today. You better get all your paperwork together. You better have the wording right. We're not bringing this family back to this courtroom. If you think you need them back, if you don't get your act together today, and you have to have them here for something else later, you'll have to deliver it to them by pigeon if that's what it takes, because we're not coming back to this courtroom. This is the way it is—no ifs, ands, or buts."

The defendants got it. The judge gave them orders about when and how the settlement would be paid. They had to pay in three payments. The first one, the smallest of the three, would come within two weeks of that day. The rest of it would be paid over a three-month period. He said that was the way it was going to be.

A couple of weeks later, one of the defendant's lawyers decided he didn't have the wording correct about Carney. He claimed that the way it was written left Carney able to come back on them in the future. We were in San Antonio at the time—in October 2009—for Jack's surgeries, and I didn't know what I was supposed to do about this.

Jack

I said to A'Leta, "Tell Chris, 'You heard what the judge said,' and then you let him handle it."

Chris called Judge Wesley. The next day, an attorney came to the house we had rented in San Antonio (to recover from surgery) and had us sign something. Judge Wesley had told the defendants, "You're not returning to this courtroom. I don't care who can come back on you in the future. That's your problem. You should've had it together when I told you."

A'Leta

Several weeks later, we went to court for a hearing that dealt with Carney. During the hearing, Judge Wesley motioned Carney to come up to the bench. He turned his computer around and let her play games. Then he started laughing while court was in session. "By the way, in case you're wondering, she just scored a high score on 'Hannah Montana,'" he explained.

Afterwards, we went up to the judge to thank him for doing so much for our family.

"I want you to know that the card you sent me is the best thing I have ever gotten," he said. "I carry it with me wherever I go. I show it to everybody who will read it. It is the best gift I have ever received."

It's funny, but I don't remember the exact words I wrote on the thank-you card I'd sent him earlier. I remember thanking him for being obedient to what God wanted him to do, and how he had changed our family's life—things like that. You know, when God's speaking to you and through you, you don't remember half of what you say.

The judge said, "It will be framed in my office." Then he ended our visit by telling us, "I'll be here for you, for whatever you need."

Afterwards, a clerk called Jack over. "I want you to know that's never happened before. Nobody's ever sat with him up here, or played on his computer."

Jack said, "Well, I guess she's just like her mama."

Carney just looked at us with an expression that said, "Whatever!"

I have to say this about how the lawsuit was adjudicated: Jack's case was not normal. All kinds of little details could have influenced or caused a different outcome. But God had his hand in every bit of it, from start to finish.

OUR ROMANCE

A'Leta

When Jack was in the hospital and in the rehabilitation center, counselors worked with him on his depression. It was something he and the rest of us had to fight every minute of every day. Depression for burn patients is completely normal. I found an article about a Johns Hopkins study that followed more than two hundred long-term burn patients. Forty-six percent of those showed signs of depression and—I have to say—that sounds low to me. As one of the study organizers states, therapy for burn patients should help them not only improve their ability to function, but their "ability to feel better about themselves, both of which are equally important."[32]

John Findley, a psychiatrist for the burn and trauma unit at Massachusetts General Hospital, comments on one of the burn patient's unique issues—the way they look. "It isn't possible to change society's reaction to disfigured people. But we can get (patients) to look at themselves differently, look beyond the skin and see the healthy person that was there before the injury."

In some ways, these comments state the obvious. I do think they're true, though. I also think they apply to the burn survivor's family. We need to remember what they were like before tragedy robbed them of what they looked like, many of the things they were able to do, and in some ways even their personalities. The problem with looking back to the past and living only with memories is that it can depress not only the patient but his loved ones too. The challenge is to remember but not dwell on what once was, but on the reality of the present, while at the same time encouraging when we see glimmers of our "old" loved one.

The reason for these facts is to make it easier to relate with us and with others that you may know. In Jack's case, his therapists tried to get him to "face reality" by telling him that I would probably ask him for a divorce, or that I would get tired of all the stress or being the caregiver, and I would simply abandon him. Apparently, this behavior is the expected reaction.

How sad! Okay, I admit it—I am a "good little Baptist church-going girl," but the possibility of divorce never occurred to me. I hope it's obvious in my journal entries that I would have never done that. It wasn't what I believed was right. Not only that, but Jack was *Jack*, the man I had always loved. I do not believe love dies as a result of a tragedy or any other life-altering event

At the same time, I admit there were many days when I didn't think I could keep going. Some days I began to get glimpses of my "Big Sexy," as I have always called him. But other days were very dark.

Friday, April 27, 2007

Yesterday, Jack and I celebrated our tenth wedding anniversary. He really made the effort to make it as special if not more special than the last ones. Anything is better than last year, considering Jack was in ICU and did not even know if he was in the world. I am so happy that he is able to do what he is doing now. I thank God every day for the time that we have been given together. It has been very hard at times and stressful, to say the least, but we are blessed with family, friends, and a beautiful daughter. Carney has a lot of issues, but we are just trying to love her and be patient. We love her more than life itself, and we pray that she can get through all of this and be able to function well in society.

Tuesday, July 3, 2007

It is 11:16 p.m. and I cannot go to sleep because I cannot stop crying. My heart really hurts, and it is broken. I am scared that it will stay broken forever. Time does not heal. I wonder if I will ever feel complete again. I wonder if I will ever feel my husband's touch again or ever feel the way he made me feel from the day we met, February 14, 1994, until March 3, 2006. I want to feel—inside and out—that feeling that words cannot explain. Jack is the man that God planned for me before my birth, and God knew then that I would be where I am today. He has been preparing me since birth for this tragic event that has taken place in our lives.

I wonder if I am doing it the way God wants me to. I am his child and every parent has dreams and hopes for their children's futures. But it does not always work out the way they planned. That child may take a different path or make a decision that altered or changed the path to God's plan.

I do not want to disappoint anyone, especially God or my family. I want to make the right choices and be the best wife and mother that I can possibly be. I know this will never go away, it will just fade some eventually. This has forever changed our lives, and I can accept that. I just want the feelings of brokenness to go away, and I am scared that they never will. These feelings are feelings that someone else has placed on us. This is not or was not my choice for my family or for me.

I cannot watch a romantic scene on TV or see a couple out in public being affectionate towards one another. Watching them causes me to remember how broken I am and how unbroken I wished I was. Jack is my world, and I know that I am his. These feelings must be far worse than the emotions that come along with death. These emotions and feelings are still there every morning I wake up, and they are there when I go to bed at night. They are there in my dreams, and there is nothing on this earth that I can possibly do to forget about them for one moment. Everything that I do or say is based on the emotions and feelings of the horrific tragedy that occurred to my husband and family on March 3, 2006.

The day that I met Jack for the first time I knew that I had never seen anything as fine as he was. I was only fifteen, but I had those feelings then, and I still do think that I married the finest man on the face of the earth. I wish I could see the man I married again the way he was when I first met him that day. I long for his smell and his touch. I want to feel his perfect lips, the ones that God gave him when he created him. I want my old Jack to tell me that it is okay and that he will take care of everything. I want my old Jack to sit and hold me while I cry. I cannot even have a glimpse of my old Jack because there is nothing there of my old Jack. All of him has been changed or taken away completely. I need and want him to wake up in the morning and say, "Today is your day," or "Today is our day"—*our* as in "Jack and A'Leta" prior to March 3, 2006. I want my old Jack, and I wonder if there is enough time in our lifetimes to ever change that in me.

Sunday, December 1, 2007

I love you! I miss my old Jack on some days so bad I want to give up and just sit there and cry myself to death. And I do mean *death*. I will always miss my Jack until I die. If I do not see you [Jack] resemble the beautiful man that I married, I know that I will when we get to heaven. I do not care if God gives me a mansion or even a shack. I will sleep on the streets of gold if he will give me the opportunity to see, touch, and feel the man I married on April 26, 1997.

Back in July 2007 I must have been very, very down. "Time does not heal," I had written. But it does, in the smallest of ways … and those small ways add up, and so on, and so on.

I wrote the entry below two years and eight months—977 days—after the explosion on Rig 226.

Thursday, November 6, 2008

Monday of this week I was able to smell the sweetest scent that I have not been able to smell since March 1, 2006!

I have cried and begged God to give me that smell back, and I never realized how important it was. You know, experts say we are

> attracted to our spouse because of the smell that is unique to them. When Jack would work all day and come home, he had this distinct smell, and I loved it. It is probably sweat mixed with cologne—and no telling what else—but I loved it and I have cried just to be able to smell him for a moment.
>
> For the past couple of weeks I have woken up dreaming of that smell. Monday I started smelling it and this time it was not my imagination—it was *real.* It was Jack, and he was smelling like himself again. I was and still am so elated that I cannot contain myself. I discussed it with him, and he realizes that his distinct smell is coming back. I never realized until it was gone that I would miss that or that it even was something that I needed before until it was gone.
>
> To me, that smell is heaven on earth. What is probably nasty, smelly sweat to someone else is a little piece of heaven to me. I am so thankful to God that he gave that back to me even if only for a moment. Little did I realize that his smell and his mustache against my face were the most important things I would miss, even more important than his looks. It is amazing.
>
> Now I know what it is like to feel like a kid again! The excitement that a child feels over the smallest things, things that adults take for granted every day. It is to me a miracle in itself that I can smell *my* Jack. Thank you, Jesus, for loving me enough to show me the little things in life that are important and allowing me to stop and smell the roses!

I know there are days ahead when despair will darken my outlook. But as it has been before, somehow my faith in God will overcome the darkness. It might be the smallest light in a dark day, but it's a light. I can see—barely—but I can see an end to a tunnel. We may have another tunnel to get through in the future, but that day's tunnel seems to have a way out.

At the beginning of this book we inserted "our" song, Dierks Bentley's "Come a Little Closer." The lyrics express our future hopes for both of us.

I look back at how far we've come, and I see some of my notes from those darker days. They give me hope.

LIFE IN THE HIGH COUNTRY OF NORTH CAROLINA

A'Leta

Moving time. We both knew we had to do it.

I began researching different parts of the South, looking for an area that would best suit Jack's needs. We needed a climate that was dry enough, and with air that was clear enough that Jack would be able to breathe. We had to have mild temperatures because Jack cannot sweat. We needed a secluded spot and a home that suited the unique needs of a long-term burn survivor—no stairs for him to climb, and an area somewhere on the property where we could install gym equipment for him. This was not a luxury but a necessity, so that he could keep his body exercised and not lose the elasticity of his skin, especially the grafts.

The house needed to be big enough to accommodate friends, family, and medical people. They would come as often as they could to help and support us if and when we needed it. I wanted a pretty setting for Jack too, since he would be spending most of his time there. Finally, we needed a place close to a church we could attend.

People who know me are not surprised to learn where we settled into our new life. However, those who don't might wonder, why the high country? Why the mountains of western North Carolina for this family from the steamy Magnolia State? Two of us are Mississippi natives, and the third one might as well be.

First, we chose the High Country for the climate. By the time Jack had the last surgery in San Antonio that he would have for a while, I had already narrowed the possibilities down. Western North Carolina was at the top of my list. I shared the results of my search with Jack's surgeon, Dr. Wolf, and he confirmed that the area was the best place he could think of.

Second, the area's natural beauty. We fell in love with it on our first visit. We found a lovely, white-frame, 1890s farmhouse tucked into a small, green clearing a little ways up a mountain. As soon as we laid eyes on it, we knew God had led us there and that he would make it ours.

A babbling brook runs through our property. We have chickens and let our three dogs run free. It is the most peaceful place we have ever experienced. It also has the needed features for Jack's continuing rehabilitation. The home and its secluded setting have played a big part in our family's healing process. It is our "little piece of heaven." When you drive up to it, it's as if you're driving into a fairy-tale book.

Third, the house: no stairs. Well … actually, we have tons of stairs. I guess everybody has to compromise a little. We can always do future renovations to accommodate possible setbacks in the future: a big garage with a gym for Jack, and lots of bedroom space for guests.

Fourth, the people: Bethel Baptist Church. It's not close by, but it's where God led us. The church has welcomed us and loved us since the first time we visited. They get a kick out of us, with our *slooow* Southern talk. They think we are the biggest backwoods rednecks they've ever met. I think everyone else in the High Country thinks so too! They're always chuckling about our accents, our expressions, and so on. We love those people. We've been able to offer our home to the church for gatherings, and we have been blessed with wonderful new friends.

We kept Carney out of public school, and I homeschooled her beginning in fall 2009. She desperately needed peace, quiet, stability, and plain, everyday closeness with her daddy and me. She needed an atmosphere where I wasn't continually preoccupied with taking care of Jack's daily needs. Jack and I are now able to spend the much-needed time with her that she has been waiting on for so long. She started back to public school in the fall of 2010. Since our move to North Carolina, we have watched her improve daily both emotionally and socially. She is blossoming into a beautiful, godly young lady with an outgoing personality and an ability to talk to just about anyone. She is a gift from God! I pray that her heart's desire will be to know him more and to serve him all the days of her life.

The church is very supportive of Jack's ministry. They have given him opportunities to speak about his experiences, and he's developing that talent with church and community groups. He has created a website (www.Billyjackmcdaniel.com) as a way to share his story and to connect with community and church groups in the future.

When he speaks to groups, one of my favorites of Jack's statements goes something like this:

> "You know, I look like I'm hurting on the outside. But my scars on the inside are far worse and far more painful than what you see on the outside. I know there are many who are hurting on the inside. That's what God can fix. He is changing me every day, and he can change you."

Today Jack does physical and massage therapy several times a week. Surgeries will continue for years to come. It will be a lifelong process for Jack and all of our family. Thanks to his therapist, George Bunton, Jack was able to receive his therapy in our home for the first year we lived here, which made things much easier for him. George has also been a wonderful Christian friend to Jack. I guess you could say George has been not only a godsend for physical needs, but for emotional needs as well.

As for future surgeries, Jack is able to choose when and where surgeries will be done. He needs some in the future, maybe even as many as fifty more according to the doctors, but right now we are taking time to heal emotionally as a family and learning how to live with and appreciate this new life God has blessed us with. We have to make a conscious decision every day to live according to God's will and to allow our tragedy to bring glory to God.

As for Jack, my Big Sexy is just as sexy to me now as he ever was, despite his physical condition left by that ravaging fire, which came like a thief in the night to steal and destroy. It left him with almost no resemblance to the man who swept me off my feet when I was just fifteen years old. What makes him so sexy now is that I know I have the strongest husband on the face of the earth. No man I know, besides Jesus, has been through anything as physically or mentally painful or challenging and lived to survive. And he is not just "surviving." No, not Jack! He's living life and making the best of it that he can.

Jack is once again my safety net when everything else is a chaotic mess. He wraps me up in his arms, and I bury my face in his broad chest and just breathe. I look into his big, brown, beautiful eyes and I can still see "my Jack," Billy Jack McDaniel, Jr. We still have the fairy-tale romance all little princesses dream about. The good Lord is the only one who gets the glory for that. Without Jesus as Lord of our lives and our household, we would have a much different tale to offer the world.

Jack faces more surgeries in the future. His hands need work, and he'll need another neck release, as well as releases on his arms, where the skin has contracted. He says he needs a brain transplant too—a comment that makes me smile at my new-yet-old Jack! These things await, and he'll get them done. We'll all be with him.

CHAPTER 27

FRIENDS IN NEED, FRIENDS IN DEED: THANKS FROM JACK AND A'LETA

A'Leta

In this life, family and friends make all the difference in a person's ability to handle hard times. There were times when our families and friends shot a few blanks when it came to being the best kind of help, but without them neither of us could have made it through the long days and nights and the decisions we had to make. They supported me with shoulders to lean on; they sat in Jack's room, sometimes with me, but others times they sat without me so I could get a break; they prayed with us; they helped me bandage Jack or attend his personal needs; and they joked and laughed with us, sharing that southern humor and news about home that broke the tension for us Mississippi rednecks.

I need to turn back the calendar pages a few years to describe my best friend and business partner, Shelley Harrison. A couple of years after Carney was born, I took a break from the health care field, where I was employed as a Certified Medical Assistant. I did something completely different—I went to "nail school" and got my certification. My longtime friend, Shelly, was a hair stylist. A week before I finished nail school, Shelley decided to leave the salon where she was working and go out on her own.

Shelley and I rented a one-room shop from a friend and church member. It was out in the country, and we even had donkeys in the back of the store. We painted and fixed it up, and I bought a nail table for $25. We named our shop Hello Beautiful.

In 2005 and several moves later, we had each built up a large clientele, so rented new space in Florence, Mississippi. We expanded our shop to include accessories and shoes. Jamie, another friend who had a shop in Florence, joined us, along with Brittany, a sweet, local high school student. They always talked "smack" about how many times a day Jack sometimes called. It was all in fun, and I fed it right back to them. Shelley and I agreed from the beginning that we would try our best to establish a fun atmosphere for our clients, and we would not participate in the usual "beauty shop gossip." We weren't perfect, but we did a pretty good job of sticking to our guns.

Our own rule didn't keep us, our shop, or the girls working for us from being part of the gossip at other shops in town. That is a whole other book in itself. Those were fun times! Hello Beautiful is still there and thriving today, though not as fun or eventful with me not there. I am proud of Shelley and how she has grown and made successful what we started together.

Shelley's help didn't end with the business, either. She visited Jack and me at the hospital so many times I can't count them, along with her husband, Stephen. They arrived at LSU Medical Center on March 4, 2006, about an hour after I got there. They were around for Jack and me during the darkest days of our lives. Even though we now live ten hours apart, I can call Shelley day or night, and I have no doubt she would be there for me. And her ability to make me laugh? That's worth a fortune!

She wrote us an e-mail soon after the rig disaster, which expresses her love and sense of humor:

> I believe you both know I love you soooo much, but what I want to tell you is how proud I am of both of you. Y'all have shown such a strong bond for each other and for God. I know God has a plan

in mind and it is sooo big. And now all we can do is wait and pray for God to continue his miracles he is performing in Jack. A'Leta, I want you to know how much our friendship means to me … I catch myself looking out the window for your car to come flying into the parking lot. I never would have imagined I would go through withdrawals from you …

And Jack, all those many, many times the phone rang at the shop and we would pick on A'Leta because it was you again! Now I can't wait for the phone to ring and see your number on the caller ID … How many people can say they can call their best friend's husband and talk about everything with them? Not too many. I know God will soon let my phones ring with both of you on the line. Just keep lifting God's holy name up and remembering how much he loves you and that everything happens for a reason.

Love, Shelley

Later during that first month, after a visit, she sent me these words:

A'Leta, I had to leave you tonight, and you think it would get easier but I do believe it is harder every time. Remember, though, I am here for whatever you need. I am so proud of Jack. He is doing so well. You can tell God is working when you see Jack look at you with those lovesick puppy eyes he has for you. Y'all have such a great love for each other and God, and I know he will continue to bless Jack during his recovery. Just like you said, you and God have an understanding, and you will not settle for anything less than 100%, and I know that's what God will give you … I love both of you sooooooo much. Shelley

On Easter 2006 we got a special note from her. Here's part of it:

Hey y'all! I have been thinking a lot about y'all today. On this special day we think of what Jesus did for us on the cross and how much he suffered, and I can't help but think of you …

She kept those e-mails coming often. She didn't forget Jack's birthday on May 14, and she combined it with a Mother's Day wish:

> HAPPY BIRTHDAY TO YOU!!! Jack, I love you so much and I hope you had a wonderful birthday. It was so wonderful to see you and hear you talk to us and cut up with us. You are a strong man and I can't wait to see you soon.
>
> A'Leta, HAPPY MOTHER'S DAY to a strong, loving, and giving mother. You are also an inspiration to many—never thought I'd be saying that!! But you are and I love you. Get some rest and remember we are all here praying.
>
> Love, Shelley

Another childhood friend, Ellen Jolly, Shelley's cousin, sacrificed her family time to take care of our family. Her husband, Brian, took care of our home and yard from the time Jack got hurt for about a year and a half. Not to mention all the little things that I depended on him to do or to help me with! It is hard living like a single parent. Yet, I could call on Brian day or night to take care of the "honey-dos" that Jack did so well before he was burned. Ellen took Carney to school every day that I was in the hospital with Jack. Ellen dealt with Carney's laughter, tears, meltdowns, and silent treatments as she and Carney were in the car together. I know a lot of those were mentally exhausting. I am grateful that Ellen was there to minister to Carney in those very dark moments.

We heard often from many other friends, church members, coworkers, and family members. We also received e-mails and cards from people we didn't even know, people who had heard about Jack and me and wanted to express their willingness to pray for us or help us in any way they could.

Our employee Brittany sent a sweet e-mail:

> I came to know and love [you] in such a short time. It's not the same at work without A'Leta there to give me orders or Jack around to call every five minutes, or Carney there to beg me to play with her! … You guys are by far the strongest family that I've ever known.

My parents offered their own words of encouragement soon after that night:

> Thank you for wearing your faith like a badge—it looks real good ... We know that God is with you both, especially in Jack's ICU room, which makes that a holy place ... Being in God's presence while he is working is a very humbling experience.

On April 26, our anniversary and a very trying time for both of us, they wrote a note:

> We just wanted to tell you "Happy Anniversary," and we hope that you are going to have a great day. There are so many people who love you and Jack, and so many of those have been lifting you up in daily prayers and doing all they could to make you more comfortable under such trying and stressful situations ... The road ahead is not going to be easy, but God is not going to abandon you now. He will not give you any task that he will not prepare you to finish beautifully. Don't worry, you and Jack have been wrapped in God's arms from day one, and he has really been strutting his stuff in Shreveport, Louisiana. Keep on smiling, and remember how special you are to us. Carney is still asleep and she is so beautiful. I hate to wake up the little angel. Ha! She is so "groany"—can't imagine where she got that! She will be fine—God is still taking care of her ...
>
> We love you, Daddy and Mama

Daddy and Mama didn't just say they loved us—they showed it by being with us in Shreveport or wherever else we needed them, and by keeping Carney without complaining. They kept us on the church's prayer list, and many of those praying people also sent us regular e-mails. My sisters and brother came to visit too, and they and their kids wrote us often.

Jack's family was good too. He had not had a good relationship with his daddy before the oil-rig incident, but his daddy put any bad feelings behind him and visited him regularly. So did his stepbrother, Chad, and his mama. His mother had a hard time seeing Jack in the condition he was in, and I had some sharp words with her a couple of times about keeping her feelings in check when she went into his room. But I can't imagine how she was feeling. After all, Jack is her only child.

Jack's good friend Josh was his usual, funny self. He and I "got into it" at one point, but he even colored my hair for me. Now, that's a friend!

There were many others who came and sat with us, prayed for us, and gave money to a fund set up at a local bank in Jack's name. What a blessing! Sometimes you don't know who your friends are until you really need them, and we found we had many. We were blessed with such a generous and loving group of friends, community, and church family.

They were all called by God to minister to us unselfishly, and they did just that.

IN MEMORIAM: THOUGHTS ABOUT A SENSELESS TRAGEDY

Jack

The Deepwater Horizon explosion and resulting environment disaster is still making news. There are few people in the United States, England, and even throughout the world who have not heard about it. It has probably turned into the biggest environmental disaster in US history. At the time of this writing, we don't know the long-term effects yet to be seen in the waterfowl, the fish, and the underwater and beach front plant life. Cleanup still continues, as it should.

The realities that are not being reported often anymore, though, are the effects of the disaster on the families who lost loved ones. That will be felt for the rest of their lives. They are still recuperating from injuries, facing job losses, and trying to handle issues that don't stop just because the news stories are no longer appearing on the channels.

Not long ago, a TV news story reported that the typical payout thus far by the government to these families has been a little more than $12,000.[33] Is this a joke? How far is that going to go? I won't even try to answer. We know the answer already.

What is the value of a human life? Each of the eleven men who died in seconds on the Deepwater Horizon rig was some mother's son. Many left behind wives, children, brothers, sisters, mothers, fathers, friends … and on and on. These were men made in the image of God, and they were beloved of God, just as I am, my family is, and you are. I do not want them to be forgotten.

To honor those men, I list their names here:

Anderson, Jason. b. Nov. 22, 1974, d. Apr. 20, 2010
Burkeen, Aaron Dale. b. Apr. 24, 1972, d. Apr. 20, 2010
Clark, Donald, Sr. b. unknown, d. Apr. 20, 2010
Curtis, Stephen Ray. b. Jul. 11, 1969, d. Apr. 20, 2010
Jones, Gordon Lewis. b. Jun. 26, 1981, d. Apr. 20, 2010
Kemp, Roy Wyatt. b. Jan. 21, 1983, d. Apr. 20, 2010
Kleppinger, Karl, Jr. b. Aug. 21, 1971, d. Apr. 20, 2010
Manuel, Keith Blair. b. Aug. 3, 1953, d. Apr. 21, 2010
Revette, Dewey Allen. b. May 27, 1961, d. Apr. 20, 2010
Roshto, Shane Michael. b. Nov. 23, 1987, d. Apr. 20, 2010
Weise, Adam T. b. Jan. 19, 1986, d. Apr. 20, 2010

My goal is to make such an impact that you never forget; maybe to say something you don't want to forget. I understand depression. I was sitting at my table in Florence, Mississippi, with a Bible in front of me and a gun just to the side. I had made the decision that I was going to find comfort one way or the other.

I opened the Bible to where Jesus was crucified. Jesus a Savior? Yes. I also read where he was a man first. He took on all pain and sin in an instant. He did not quit. If *he* felt all the world's pain at once—and just my pain is enough to kill a man—and did not quit, well then, I could manage mine. My pain medicine dose has not increased in years. God has given me comfort, and I want to spread that.

I also want to spread the safety aspect of my incident. I am the blood, the fact that every safety policy is written in blood. I can make a huge impact if only given the chance.

When we hear another story about tragedy of any kind, may we remember to pray for the families of the survivors and to reach out to help in whatever way we can.

To God be the glory. God bless you all.

"Look what God can do!"

Billy Jack McDaniel

OUR PRAYER FOR YOU

We pray that you have been touched by this story and that it may change your life and bring you hope in your time of despair. Our prayer is that God's glory, grace, and mercy have been shown to you throughout every page of this book. We want you to know there is a hope and an eternal future when it seems our days could not get any darker or our pain be any less bearable.

God sent his one and only precious Son to make sure that we can have an eternal life that is free of pain, guilt, sorrow, illness, and everything else that we experience here on this earth.

The following scriptures show you the only way to the Father:

> For all have sinned and fall short of the glory of God.
>
> —Romans 3:23

> But God demonstrates his own love for us in this: While we were still sinners, Christ died for us.
>
> —Romans 5:8

> For the wages of sin is death, but the gift of God is eternal life in Christ Jesus our Lord.
>
> —Romans 6:23

> That if you confess with your mouth, "Jesus is Lord," and believe in your heart that God raised him from the dead, you will be saved.
>
> —Romans 10:9

> Everyone who calls on the name of the Lord will be saved.
>
> —Romans 10:13

We want to hear from you about how God has used our family to possibly change yours. Please let us know how God is being glorified. After all, that is the most important thing on this earth!

Billy Jack McDaniel: BillyJack@billyjackmcdaniel.com
A'Leta Combs McDaniel: Aleta@billyjackmcdaniel.com
Aleana@billyjackmcdaniel.com
Visit our website: www.billyjackmcdaniel.com

Jack is available for speaking engagements and interviews.

Shortly after my injury, I introduced my cousin Chris McDaniel to Pastor Lee Yancey, who was our minister at the time. Both are Republicans, and both were running at the same time (from district districts) for the Mississippi State Senate. Both are conservative, believed in God, and believed that if you don't try, you're not going to succeed at anything. God never said, "Now that you're saved, sit there, and I'll give it to you." He always says, "Let's go. Let's get up. Let's go." They both believed that.

Chris and Lee hit it off, and they were both elected to the senate that year. Chris went to work right away, doing everything he could to help the people of the great state of Mississippi, at the same time making a name for himself in political circles.

Jack

To my wife, A'Leta:

Babygirl, I love you so much. I cannot tell how sorry I am that you had to go through this. I know I treated you so badly at times that you should have left me. I am so thankful you didn't. I cannot imagine a day without you with me. I can know the strength you found to do the things you did. It took your life, your emotions, and your thoughts and twisted them into a spiral of confusion. I am so proud of you and wanted to tell you. People ask me about my wife, and I describe you as an oak tree standing in a field of pines.

Thank you, and always know that whatever happens I love you and thank you so much. I don't think a spouse should ever have to endure what you had to endure. I hope that women and men both learn from your dedication, love, and commitment to God. You took your vows to heart, and I can only hope that I could be as strong as you are.

Remember, Babygirl, I love you!

To my child, Carney:

Carney bug, I love you so much, baby. I am so proud of you, and to see you blossoming now is amazing. You have something that very few have, and I hope you use it to become stronger and stronger. I remember when you were a baby and would not sleep unless you were on my chest. Then, when I first came home from the hospital, you would sleep with us some. Once you went to sleep, you would snuggle up and lay your head on my shoulder. The doctors told me that I had to make you stop that. I just laughed at them and said if that caused me to die then I would die. I loved it so much. I wanted to be your daddy so much and I couldn't. I wanted to protect you, and you were protecting me. You and your mother are so strong and so much alike that it's not even funny.

Thank you for being my child, my Boo, the thing I held on to every day, and sometimes the only reason I tried. Please remember that your daddy loves you and wants only the best for you. You have come around in the last year or so and now want me to do everything and be there for everything. When you laugh it brings joy to my heart. There was a time when you didn't laugh at all. I know you have heard me say that I wish I could feel you kiss me on my cheek just one more time, I do. It is something you can't understand until you have children of your own. Thank you for all the kisses you gave and continue to give. Thank you for the strength and inspiration.

Daddy loves you with all his heart.

ENDNOTES

1. According to "How to Get a Good Job Working On An Offshore Oil Drilling Rig" on eHow.com, a worm may be asked to paint, sandblast, carry bags of drilling mud, do all the lowest jobs. Any new crew member with no experience starts out as a worm. As the article states, "Don't be offended, everyone on the rig was once a worm themselves."
2. Tripping pipe is the physical act of pulling the drill string out of the well bore and then running it back in. This is done by breaking out or disconnecting (when pulling out of the hole) *every other 2 or 3 joints of drill pipe* at a time (called a "stand") and racking them vertically in the derrick. When feasible, the driller will start each successive trip on a different "break" so that after several trips, fresh pipe dope will have been applied (when running back in the hole) to every segment of the drill string. Tripping pipe is often done to replace a worn-out drill bit, though there are many problems that might call for the tripping of pipe. Down hole tools such as MWD (measurement while drilling), LWD (logging while drilling), or mud motors break down quite often. Another common reason for

tripping is to replace damaged drill pipe. It is important to get the pipe out of the well bore quickly and safely before it can snap. See Wikipedia, http://en.wikipedia.org/wiki/Tripping_(pipe).

3. Rubber disk surrounding drill pipe or tubing that removes mud as the pipe is brought out of the hole, or the pressure-sealing element of a stripper blowout preventer. See http://oilgasglossary.com/?s=stripper+rubber.
4. Well logging that incorporates measurement tools into the drillstring and provides real-time information to help with steering the drill. See *Rigzone,* www.rigzone.com/training/insight.asp?insight_id=296&c_id=1.
5. Tool pushers are in charge of keeping the rig in all necessary tools, equipment, and supplies. A tool pusher is a rig supervisor. See http://en.wikipedia.org/wiki/Tool_pusher.
6. Something I didn't quite understand during those hours but know now: God placed those nurses—Mrs. Debbie, Terri, and Shannon, among others, to be a part of an amazing plan that God began the day he made me to be Billy Jack McDaniel's help mate. "And the LORD God said 'It is not good that man should be alone; I will make him a helper comparable to him'" (Gen. 2:18, NKJV).
7. According to Merriam-Webster's Collegiate Dictionary, a *tracheostomy* is the surgical formation of an opening into the trachea through the neck, especially to allow the passage of air. It can be a long-term solution, as it was with Jack. It is often abbreviated *trach,* and that's the way it'll often appear in this book. A *tracheotomy* is the surgical operation of cutting into the trachea, especially through the skin. It's done often as an emergency procedure. Medical personnel often abbreviate it as *trache.* The EMT did a *trache* on Jack while he was in the ambulance.
8. I think of Jesus, who loved children so much: "After taking them in His arms, He laid His hands on them and blessed them" (Mark 10:16 HCSB).
9. I need to clarify that for several weeks I was not actually able to express these worries since I was still intubated. I couldn't talk, just grunt or gesture, until the nurses made me an alphabet board. But believe me when I say I communicated these feelings one way or

the other. I was convinced—and I tried to get them to understand what I "knew" was happening.

10. Volume 2, Issue 29, July 30, 2007, http://www.psychweekly.com/aspx/article/ArticleDetail.aspx?articleid=542.
11. I had *eighty-two blood transfusions* while I was in the hospital.
12. I wrote this first entry two days after Jack had been brought to LSUHospital.
13. This entry covers the day's events for Sunday, March 5.
14. This was just a little tiff that didn't last long, and I "unfired" him soon after.
15. The first grafts were pig skin. They were used while a specialty laboratory grew "cultured skin," which is typically grown from the patient's own skin. From a piece of the patient's own skin that is small as a postage stamp a laboratory can grow skin that can cover large areas. It does have its limitations and it takes three weeks or so to grow it, but from a practical standpoint it works much better long-term for extensively burned patients than skin grafts from the patient himself or from another donor.
16. "Mammaw" was what we called my grandmother on my mother's side. Her maiden name was Carney. She was a huge help to us, stepping in to watch Carney when my mother couldn't. She passed away in 2007.
17. Zyprexa (olanzapine) is usually prescribed for schizophrenia or similar conditions. In Jack's case, it was given to help him with the hallucinations and PTSD symptoms he was having. Ativan, or lorazazepam, relieves anxiety.
18. I need to clarify how Jack was communicating. Often when I say "he told me" or "he said," he was using the alphabet board the nurses had made him to spell things out. He still had an intubation tube in his throat and could only croak out a few words. Communication was difficult, though we learned to do it—we had to.
19. Haldol (haloperidol) is an antipsychotic that is supposed to help a patient distinguish between things or ideas that are real and those that are not real. It's often used with Alzheimers and dementia patients.

20. A blowout preventer is a large, specialized valve used to seal, control and monitor oil and gas wells. Blowout preventers were developed to cope with extreme erratic pressures and uncontrolled flow (formation kick) emanating from a well reservoir during drilling. Kicks can lead to a potentially catastrophic event known as a blowout. Blowout preventers are critical to the safety of crew, rig (the equipment system used to drill a wellbore), and environment, and to the monitoring and maintenance of well integrity; thus blowout preventers are intended to be fail-safe devices. I guess it's obvious that the blowout preventer on Rig 226 was not fail-safe. See *Wikipedia,* http://en.wikipedia.org/wiki/Blowout_preventer.
21. Demerol (medperidine) is a narcotic analgesic similar to morphine, used to relieve moderate to severe pain. It works by changing the way the body senses pain.
22. Phenergan (promethazine) is used to relieve the symptoms of allergic reactions such as allergic rhinitis (runny nose and watery eyes caused by allergy to pollen, mold, or dust), allergic conjunctivitis (red, watery eyes caused by allergies), allergic skin reactions, and allergic reactions to blood or plasma products.
23. We did eventually take his advice. I homeschooled her for one year, but not that following fall.
24. From *Scandinavian Journal of Trauma, Resuscitation, and Emergency Medicine* online, inputted from Vittorio Pavoni, Lara Gianesello, Laura Paparella, Laura TadiniBuoninsegni, and Elisabetta Barboni, "Outcome predictors and quality of life of severe burn patients admitted to intensive care unit," Department of Critical Medical-Surgical Area, Section of Anesthesia and Intensive Care, Largo Palagi, 50139 Firenze, Italy, 27 April 2010, open access article at http://www.ncbi.nlm.nih.gov/pmc/articles/PMC2873368/.
25. A quick, non-technical definition: a neck release uses one of several different procedures to deal with the contraction and tightening of skin that often takes place as burn wounds heal. This is very common, especially around the neck area, and it can force a patient to hold his or her head in a stiff, uncomfortable way if not repaired. It's often done in stages, as it was with Jack, and sometimes it has to be done more than once.

26. A potent synthetic narcotic pain reliever, often used in chronic pain management. It should have worked, but it didn't on the trip back home.
27. In burn patients who are burned in the neck and shoulders areas, the neck skin tends to contract, which can pull the chin, cheeks, and lower lip so that the patient cannot bite properly. Under severe conditions the patient's breathing can be affected or the cervical spine can be distorted. Not taking care of this problem can be life-threatening.
28. Burn patients can't store fat in places they suffered severe burns. The only place on Jack that could store fat was his belly. Because of that, the fat had built up to the point where he was having trouble breathing. In the procedure, the doctors removed the fat and put it in other places, but it didn't take.
29. The account here is true, though we cannot reveal some details since the settlement details legally, to benefit the McDaniel Family, will be kept confidential. We have also changed the name of the judge for privacy and legal reasons. Otherwise, we describe what happened in that court as we remember it.
30. This is my paraphrase of the judge's words. The details are as I remember them, and someone else might remember them a little differently.
31. The citation system that law students, lawyers, scholars, judges, and other legal professionals follow.
32. University of Michigan social worker, quoted in *General Hospital Psychiatry* journal, Elsevier Science, at http://www.medicalnews-today.com/articles/60735.php, accessed 05 March 2011.
33. http://news.yahoo.com/s/ap/20110302/ap_on_bi_ge/us_gulf_oil_spill_claims.

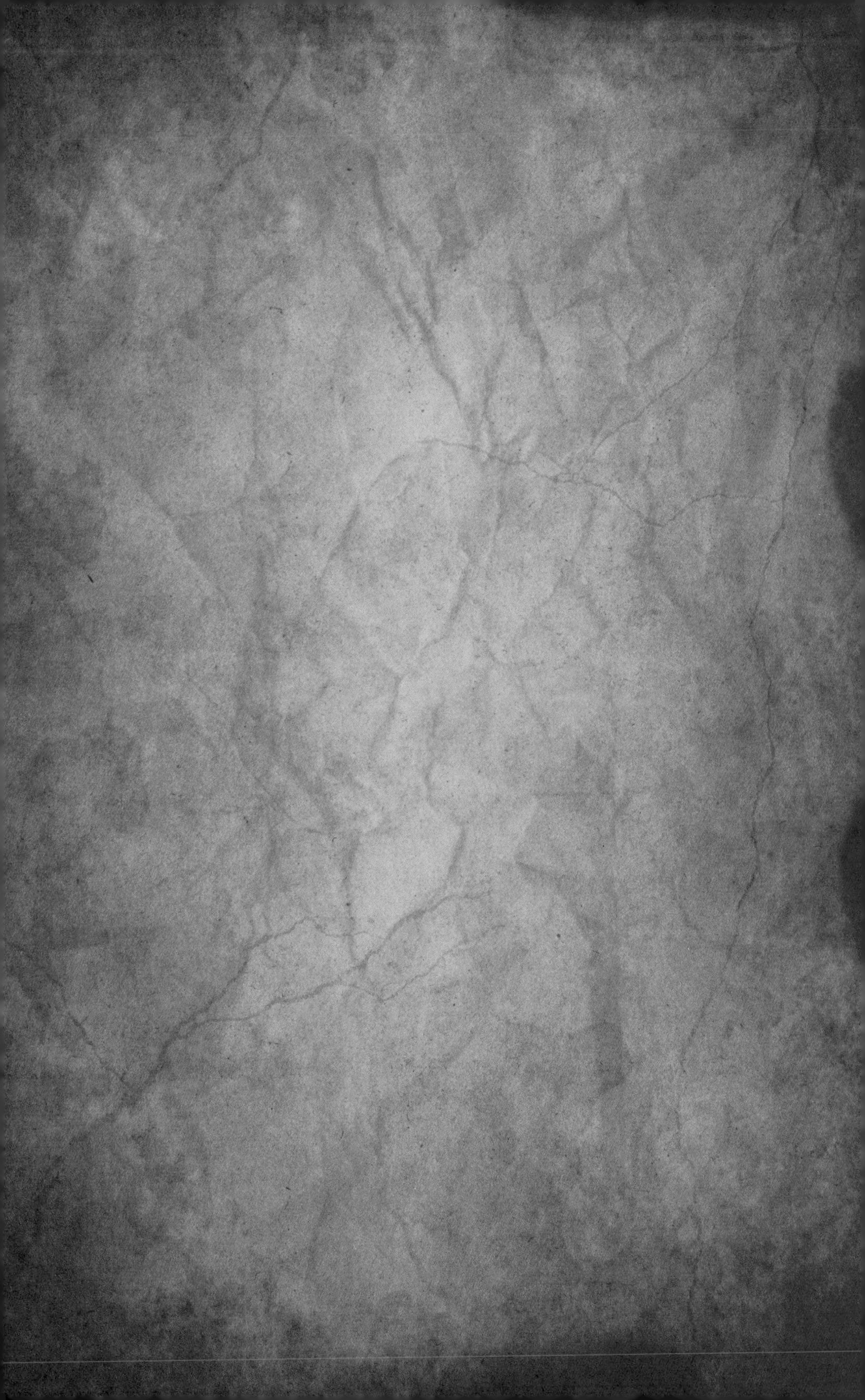

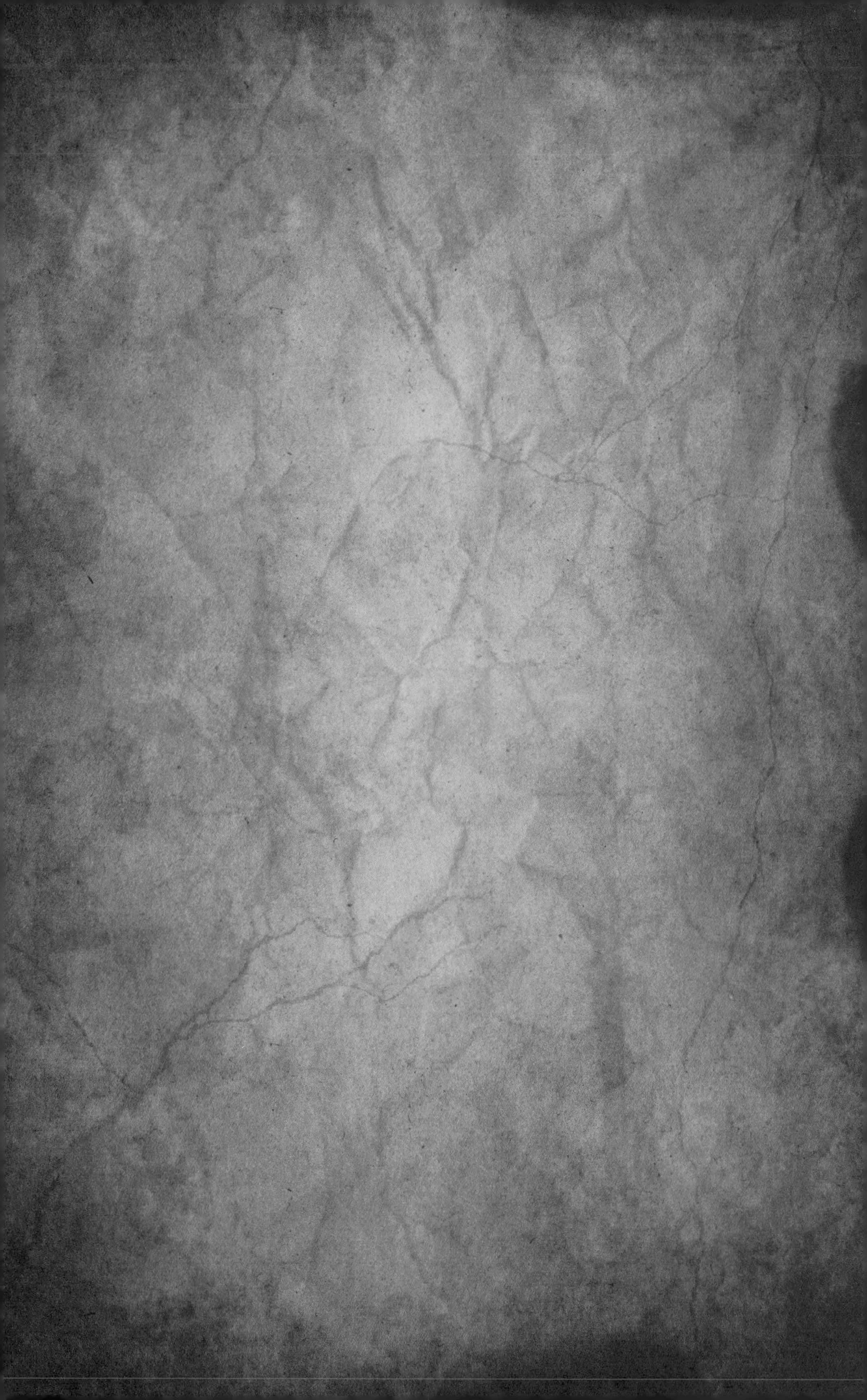